HELLVEN

THE STRUGGLES OF BEING A WORLDLY CHRISTIAN

DAVID STANFIELD

Hellven: The Struggles of Being a Worldly Christian

Trilogy Christian Publishers A Wholly Owned Subsidiary of Trinity Broadcasting Network

2442 Michelle Drive Tustin, CA 92780

Cover design by: Trilogy Christian Publishing

For information about special discounts for bulk purchases, please contact Trilogy Christian Publishing.

Manufactured in the United States of America

10 9 8 7 6 5 4 3 2 1

Library of Congress Cataloging-in-Publication Data is available.

ISBN: 978-1-68556-589-3

E-ISBN: 978-1-68556-590-9

DEDICATION

I dedicate this book to my son, Donovan Stanfield, who lost his worldly fight on March 21, 2016. I love you and miss you every day, son.

Matthew 5:16 ;

TABLE OF CONTENTS

INTRODUCTION

First of all, I want to introduce myself to you. I am just a normal guy, a son, a husband, and a father. I was raised as one of four children to a preacher, so needless to say, I grew up in the church. From as young as I can remember, I was always at church every time the doors were open. I was saved at the age of eight years old. As I have gotten older, I have always held close to the beliefs in which I was raised, but just like most people, I have always struggled with the things of this world. I am in no way perfect, and I struggle every day with all kinds of problems. I will talk about some of my own worldly struggles throughout this book, but I first want to talk about how this book came to be.

For some reason unknown to me, I am one of those people that does not very often remember dreams. If you ask me if I dream, I will typically say "no" because I just do not ever remember dreaming. On the rare occasions that I do dream, I typically dream weird things, such as inventing something, then wake up to jot down the ideas and sketch pictures of them. I have several really good ideas, but I have never done anything with them until one night. I had a dream, but I would say it was way more than a dream. In it, God spoke directly to me. He showed me in great detail the picture on the cover of this book, the format of this book, talked to me about topics for chapters of the book, and instructed me to write it. I immediately woke up, grabbed a pad and pen, and sketched out the cover as He showed me and wrote down some notes. Then I went back to sleep.

The next morning when I woke up, I thought to myself, *Was that all a dream or what?* I rolled over and found my notes and my sketch lying there. I then spoke to God and asked, "Why in the world would you ask or even want me to write a book?" I hate reading and writing and would rather have a root canal than read a book, much less write one. As a matter of fact, I have only read a book from front to back a couple of times in my whole life. In high school, I was the student who bought the cliffs notes just to pass a test over a literature assignment because I didn't want to read the actual book. Even listening to audiobooks drives me crazy and doesn't keep my attention. "So why me?" I asked. Over and over, I kept asking and throwing out all of these excuses to God. I never got an answer.

Some time passed. I had only told my wife about all of this. One day, as I was riding around with a friend of mine, for whatever reason, I told him about the experience. I didn't get to the part where I told him that I didn't know why God would ask me to write it. Before I could, my friend looked at me and said, "David, this is awesome! Do you realize that God could tell anyone in this world to write that book, but He chose you! Do you understand that if He wanted a goat to write a book, He could make it happen?" It was right then and there that I realized that God spoke through my friend to give me my answer.

So, you probably think this is the part where I tell you that I immediately sat down at the computer and started typing and working on this book. Well, it wasn't. That conversation happened five years before I began to write, and it was probably several months before that when I had the dream where God spoke to me about this book. The thoughts of the book were always in the back of my mind, and the thoughts of being disobedient to God were always there with it. I just let the things of this world take place of what was more important, which we all struggle with daily because of the shape of fallen humanity in a sin-saturated world.

I actually started writing early in 2016 and got about twelve pages written when I just stopped again. Several months went by, and I constantly had convictions about it, but I ignored them yet again. On Sunday morning of November 13, 2016, I was about to walk out the door to go to church when all of a sudden, I got an instant message from that same old friend I mentioned earlier. I hadn't actually seen him or even talked to him in about two years, and he could have no clue if I was or had begun working on this book. The message simply said, "Write the book." It really hit me hard. I just thanked him for giving me the confirmation I needed, and he responded with, "It'll release the blessings you've been waiting for." Thank you for being faithful in giving me that message, Daniel.

So much has happened in my life that has brought me to this point of obedience and actually sitting here to write consistently, but God working through that friend was a blessing. I have gone through some good and some bad things over the past several years of ignoring this calling. I often find myself wondering if the bad was due to my disobedience and what things would be like if I had just done this when I was asked to. What I have to realize is that God never went anywhere. He has patiently waited on me. I am the one who ran from His calling and decided that I was not the person for this job. In this world today, He is the only constant and consistent thing there really is. We are the ones that keep running away from Him.

Well, here I am, Lord. I will do my best, and I pray You speak through me and that I get as much out of this writing experience as someone would by reading it. I don't know if just a few close friends and family members will read this book or if You have plans for thousands of people to read it. Either way, I give You the glory for it, Lord, and will at least know I did what You asked of me.

In each chapter of this book, I will talk about some of the main struggles we live through daily. I will discuss real-life struggles that I have dealt with personally or things I have witnessed. We will dive into God's Word on each topic to see what He says we can do when faced with these struggles. Most of these struggles can be found hundreds of times in the Bible, but I will give you several verses of Scripture that you can use to help you overcome each struggle.

I pray that you will open your heart to what God has to say to you through these pages, just as I open my heart to what He wants me to say to you. I also pray that after you read the book the first time, you will continue to come back to each topic as you encounter it during your days ahead and hold fast to the promises God gives us as we struggle. God never promised us an easy life, but He does offer help to get through it and to become more than our struggles.

WHAT IS "HELLVEN"?

As Christians, we are taught that we are all sinners, and in order to receive God's gift of eternal life with Him, we must repent of our sins, believe in Jesus Christ as Savior, ask Him to cleanse us and forgive us, and come into our lives and make us new. Once we do that, we are taught that we have punched our ticket to heaven, so to speak. That ticket is a one-way pass that can't be taken away and never expires during our time here on earth. If we truly accept Christ as our Savior and fully take that experience seriously and understand it, then that so-called "ticket" will always be there for us when our time comes.

That brings us to the problem. We live in a sinful world that is full of lies and deceit. This world has gotten so corrupt and sin-filled that even Christians lose their focus on reality. We constantly fill our thoughts, hearts, and minds with things of this world that build up blinders to what really goes on around us. We have slipped so far away from the truth that we have created warped views and perceptions of the biblical beliefs that we once held close. Even some of our churches are teaching warped views of Jesus, leading congregations in the belief that Jesus is just fire insurance and not a life changer.

I believe God showed me the title of this book to help describe these warped views of how we live our lives these days. We think that just because we have been saved and have our ticket to heaven or our fire insurance, we can live our lives however we want with our remaining time here on earth without any repercussions. We think we can take a dip into sinful things and just ask for forgiveness afterward, and everything will be fine. I think current-day Christians have created a metaphorical place called "Hellven," where we think we can live here on earth knowing we are going to heaven when we die, but act and take part in sinful things like we are going to hell. We want to think that this Hellven would be the best of both worlds and that no matter what we do with our time here, we can at least make our way there afterward. A place that is not magnificent like heaven, but not near the torture of hell. A place basically just like this world we live in where we can go to church and get our "Jesus fix," but then go right back to our sinful ways afterward. A place where we can be lukewarm Christians and get away with it. I think most of us Christians today are citizens of this Hellven. We have the horns and the halo.

I'll be the first to admit that I am a citizen of Hellven. I am a sinner, and half of the people that know me wouldn't even think I am a Christian by the way I act most of the time. Unfortunately, Satan is the creator and ruler of Hellven. The Bible even refers to Satan as the prince of this world on multiple occasions. As citizens of Hellven or this world, Satan influences our thoughts, our actions, our goals, our hopes, our attitudes, our every move. He has taken control of our beliefs and education and created lies and deception at the foundation of our religion. He causes confusion and turmoil in our lives. That is why we struggle with sin so much.

How many times in your life have you been called a hypocrite or heard Christians referred to as hypocrites? Probably pretty often because of exactly what I am writing about. We Christians live so much like the world that no noticeable difference exists between us and any lost person. If we only act like Christians while at church, that means the very people that call us hypocrites are probably not there to see it. If that is the case, then they only see us when we are acting like the world, yet we are still calling ourselves Christians. Do you see the problem with this?

Let me tell you, friends: there is no such place called Hellven. Only heaven and hell. We cannot conform to this world and fall victim to Satan's deceitfulness. We have to remember and recognize that God is still sovereign and ultimately has domain over Satan and this world. The Lord wants us to make a choice when we are saved to surrender ourselves and follow Him and no longer be slaves to this world. That takes a full commitment and lots of hard work, especially these days. Let me also let you in on a secret. I fail at this daily and fail miserably at it. If you followed me through one of my typical days, you would not even think I was a Christian. I'm not proud of that. If you are honest, you would probably say you fail at it daily as well. Unfortunately, it's an epidemic we live in, and the struggle is real.

As Christians, we defeat the very purpose that God gives us by blending in with the world instead of setting ourselves apart as God wants us to. This creates an inner, spiritual struggle within our hearts. When we live in constant struggle, it is easy to become prisoners of the struggle. The good news is that we don't have to get trapped in our struggles. God can redeem us and free us of any struggles we face, and pull us out of the rut we find ourselves in if we let Him.

In order to separate yourself from the world and get yourself out of the Hellven mindset you live in, you have to first recognize that you allow Satan and this world to control you. Recognize that you let your struggles camouflage your Christianity, which makes you fit right in and look like a hypocrite. Once you see it and admit it, you can take steps toward freedom and receive forgiveness from God, and you can get back on the right path in your walk with the Lord. Your true purpose as a Christian should be to bear witness and win souls for God. It is simply hard to do this as a citizen of Hellven.

Once you start taking steps back towards God, I can guarantee you that Satan will immediately start fighting to keep you from it. Every time I take a break from writing in this book, Satan throws a hundred obstacles at me to keep me from getting back to writing. When we live in this world, it takes no effort on his part to keep you there in Hellven. But when he sees you trying to move out, that is where he spends his time and effort, so be ready. The tricky part of it all is that you can't serve your true purpose of winning souls by isolating yourself from the world, either. You still have to be in it and around it; you just can't conform to it anymore. The good news is that God promises to be with you each step of the way when we seek Him, and there is nothing in this world that we have to fear with God by our side.

> *I know your deeds, that you are neither cold nor hot. I wish you were either one or the other! So, because you are lukewarm—neither hot nor cold—I am about to spit you out of my mouth.*
>
> **Revelation 3:15–16**

> *No one can serve two masters. Either you will hate the one and love the other, or you will be devoted to the one and despise the other.*
>
> **Matthew 6:24**

> *Whoever is not with me is against me, and whoever does not gather with me scatters.*
>
> **Matthew 12:30**

> *The Spirit clearly says that in later times some will abandon the faith and follow deceiving*

spirits and things taught by demons. Such teachings come through hypocritical liars, whose consciences have been seared as with a hot iron.

1 Timothy 4:1–2

If anyone, then, knows the good they ought to do and doesn't do it, it is sin for them.

James 4:17

What good will it be for someone to gain the whole world, yet forfeit their soul? Or what can anyone give in exchange for their soul?

Matthew 16:26

Not everyone who says to me, 'Lord, Lord' will enter the kingdom of heaven, but only the one who does the will of my Father who is in heaven. Many will say to me on that day, 'Lord, Lord, did we not prophesy in your name and in your name drive out demons and in your name perform many miracles?' Then I will tell them plainly, 'I never knew you. Away from me, you evildoers!'

Matthew 7:21–23

Those who are in the realm of the flesh cannot please God.

Romans 8:8

Make a tree good and its fruit will be good, or make a tree bad and its fruit will be bad, for a tree is recognized by its fruit.

Matthew 12:33

What shall we say, then? Shall we go on sinning so that grace may increase? By no means! We are those who have died to sin; how can we live in it any longer?

Romans 6:1–2

QUESTIONING YOUR FAITH

Right off the bat, I want to jump in with a very real struggle I think many of us face and do not know how to handle: questioning your faith.

Because we live in such warped times, Satan constantly whispers in our ears and pulls us further and further away from the truth. I am certain that nearly every Christian has at one time or another questioned their faith.

Several ways exist to question our faith. The first way is questioning our actual belief in this whole "God" thing altogether. As we fail in our daily walks with God and constantly distance ourselves from Him, it becomes a huge challenge to convince ourselves that everything we were taught or learned as new Christians is real. You can easily find yourself questioning why you believe what you do at some point in your life. This can become very frustrating because, as a Christian, you feel guilty for even having those kinds of thoughts. You look to the world around you and convince yourself to explore that thought process. We constantly hear of new challenges to the Bible, or of some new religion, or some scientist that thinks they have it all figured out. There is so much confusion that can enter your thought process, which is what Satan wants. This takes Satan almost no effort to throw ideas out there that really make Christians think and question their beliefs. He probably gets a kick out of it. When you listen to things and look at all the turmoil and negativity in the world, it is sometimes just hard to believe that God would allow it all to happen.

This is something I have gone through myself on more than one occasion. As I mentioned in the preamble, I am a preacher's child, born and raised in the church. At numerous times in my adult life, I have found myself wondering where or who I would be if that were not the case. What if I was born and raised in the Middle East as a Muslim, or what if I was born into a family of non-believers that never darkened the door of a church? I wondered, would I still be a Christian now, or am I just the product of my raising? These are some deep questions that I have spent hours and days thinking about and struggling with.

I have also had interactions with people on multiple occasions where the person or people are not believers, and when they bring up certain points about why they don't believe or why the Bible can't be true, I have let my thoughts wander off and ask myself if they may be right. Or I find myself not being able to prove them wrong or direct them to Scripture that would set them straight. This type of experience can be frustrating and hard to deal with.

A second way we question our faith is by doubting if our own personal experience of salvation was real or not. Sometimes, especially for those who get saved at a very young age like me, you can question its reality. You wonder if you meant it or if you fully understood it. This can leave the door wide open for Satan to fill your head full of doubt and confusion. I was saved at eight years old and went through this very struggle at about the age of thirty. I had to seek council and come to the realization that I was indeed saved, but that I had allowed myself to become a citizen of Hellven. I let Satan fool me. I realized that I had turned from God and wandered off into the world without Him. Little did Satan know that it backfired on him and helped me straighten some things out and put me back on the right path again. It did not mean I stopped struggling, but at least I was able to seek help from God as I put my focus back on Him.

So what do these frightening questions and creeping doubts mean? Is doubting and questioning your faith a sin in itself? How do we work through and deal with these types of thoughts?

First of all, God never says that it is wrong for you to have questions or doubts, but He does give us ways to work through them. God gave us a brain and free will so that we can work through our thought processes and choose to believe or not. Unlike Satan, God will never push us or force us to believe and follow Him, but His heart's greatest desire is that we follow Him. If you struggle with believing and trusting, you need to realize that God would not tell us to do something that was not possible.

I think the biggest key to these struggles is simply faith. The definition of faith is "complete trust or confidence in someone or something." You cannot have faith without completely letting go of doubt and fully trusting in the Lord. If you call yourself a Christian, then you have to know faith is the key to our salvation. If you fully trust in God, you should be able to come to a place of full confidence in His Word. The Bible says in Romans 10:17, "Faith comes from hearing the message, and the message is heard through the word about Christ." What that verse means is that if you struggle with your faith, open up your Bible and seek the word of God through reading and studying. Open your heart to what He tells you through the Scriptures, and He will point you to what you need.

I personally think that when you find yourself questioning things and doubting your faith, you are spiritually starving. If you find yourself here, you can either feed your spirit with what it longs for, which is the Word of God, or you can continue to feed Satan with your struggles. Let me tell you: Satan has an all-you-can-eat buffet in Hellven. We all fall into this trap of his.

Besides getting into God's Word, you need to also think about your alternatives. Where would you be without your faith? Who would you be without your faith? It's probably not good. If you have truly given your heart to the Lord, even if you are not living like it now, then you have to know the feelings of conviction, and you have to see times in your life that you know without a doubt that God was with you in a certain situation. When you are saved, you invite Jesus to come into your heart and life and dwell in you. If He was not real, or He was not dwelling in you, then you wouldn't be able to feel some of the things or sense some of the things that you do in order to help you know He is there. If you can pinpoint times in your life where you know without a doubt that God was with you, then I urge you to meditate on those times and let those experiences strengthen and renew your faith. If you find it hard to find any real experiences, then I urge you to search your heart and either rededicate your life to God or just nail things down with Him again now as you may be in a better place in your life to fully understand things and fully commit to trusting in Him. Those are ways you can squash these struggles altogether. Maybe your doubt will backfire in Satan's face and actually lead you to real faith when you seek the Lord.

Jeremiah 29:13 says, "You will seek me and find me when you seek me with all your heart." Tune out Satan's lies and those whispers you hear from this world that make you doubt your faith and turn your attention to seeking the Lord and His Word. Pray and ask God to focus your thoughts on the things He wants for you.

> *For it is by grace you have been saved, through faith—and this is not from yourselves, it is the gift of God.*
>
> **Ephesians 2:8**

> *Examine yourselves to see whether you are in the faith; test yourselves. Do you not realize that Christ Jesus is in you—unless, of course, you fail the test?*
>
> **2 Corinthians 13:5**

> *Be merciful to those who doubt.*
>
> **Jude 1:22**

> *For no one can lay any foundation other than the one already laid, which is Jesus Christ.*
>
> **1 Corinthians 3:11**

> *Therefore I tell you, whatever you ask for in prayer, believe that you have received it, and it will be yours.*
>
> **Mark 11:24**

> *'For my thoughts are not your thoughts, neither are your ways my ways,' declares the LORD. 'As the heavens are higher than the earth, so are my ways higher than your ways and my thoughts than your thoughts.'*
>
> **Isaiah 55:8–9**

And without faith it is impossible to please God, because anyone who comes to him must believe that he exists and that he rewards those who earnestly seek him.

Hebrews 11:6

If any of you lacks wisdom, you should ask God, who gives generously to all without finding fault, and it will be given to you. But when you ask, you must believe and not doubt, because the one who doubts is like a wave in the sea, blown and tossed by the wind.

James 1:5–6

What we have received is not the spirit of the world, but the Spirit who is from God, so that we may understand what God has freely given us.

1 Corinthians 2:12

'For I know the plans I have for you,' declares the LORD, 'plans to prosper you and not to harm you, plans to give you hope and a future. Then you will call on me and come and pray to me, and I will listen to you. You will seek me and find me when you seek me with all your heart.

Jeremiah 29:11–13

ANGER

If you want to talk about a struggle that leads to even more problems and sin, then let's talk about anger. Think about all the problems, fights, or arguments that you have had in your life. I bet most of them have started with anger. I think of anger as a tornado. Anger creeps in and gets you all worked up, and before you know it, things are spinning out of control. It destroys everything it touches. When you are controlled by anger, you will do things and say things that will hurt your relationships. You may physically or mentally scar others leaving memories that may not ever go away. Anger can tear apart relationships and can lead you to dark places in your life.

Counselors across the world will tell you that at least 50 percent of people who come in for counseling are dealing with anger, so I know that this is a real struggle for most people, especially considering the number of people that just won't get help for it. I think it is safe to say that everyone experiences anger and struggles with it from time to time. It is a natural thing that is built into our being, and because we live in a sinful place like Hellven, anger is one of Satan's favorite tools because he can use it to create so much turmoil in our lives.

In my family, on my dad's side, we jokingly talk about the "Stanfield anger." It goes from me to my dad, back to his dad and brother, and beyond. We are all kindhearted, quiet men, but we tend to hold our emotions inside and are good at hiding them. It is hard for us to realize we are doing it most of the time, but when that happens, anger can build up and grow until it finally explodes out of you. Then the anger can look and sound greatly magnified because you didn't deal with it before it grew out of control. When you see a quiet and gentle man whom you would not expect that sort of thing from, exploding with anger, it is even more shocking and easily remembered. Unfortunately, that is what we Stanfield men have had to watch for and try to control. My grandpa was a great Christian man, but he was known to have some moments of going off on someone. Anyone who knew him could tell some stories about some sort of outburst from him. They would probably laugh about it now, but when it happened, it was shocking. Since my dad was such a strong man of God and a preacher, he was able to keep his anger in check, but he still had his moments; they just might not have been as dramatic as my grandpa's.

Personally, I find myself getting angry pretty easily, especially when going through stressful times in my life, which I have had for a while now. Little things like traffic or people being loud when all I want is a little quiet will set me off like a bomb. I will get all worked up over nothing if I let myself. There are many instances that I have let anger control me that I can look back on, which embarrass me now. One time recently, I was at a restaurant for lunch with a couple of coworkers, and we had just finished eating lunch. As we went out to get into my truck to leave, someone had parked so close to my truck that I could not even walk between the back of the vehicles to get in. I had to walk all the way around to the front and then squeeze in-between them and just barely made it inside. By the time I did make it, I was already boiling with anger towards a person that I didn't even know and had not even seen. I then proceeded to open my truck door very fast and hard, right into the vehicle parked next to me, which put a dent in it that was about a foot long. I then peeled out and yelled a few choice words before catching a glimpse at my coworker's face. He stared at me as if he didn't know who I was. I snapped out of it then and felt a little embarrassed. The scary part is that it also felt a little good. I think that it is absolutely the devil that puts that feeling of relief and pleasure in your mind in a situation like that, which only fuels the anger. He wants us to feel pleasure from it so we will continue to do it and let it control us. The embarrassment and guilt come from the Lord, which is what we have to recognize and concentrate on.

I can tell you that with my family, I think my dad recognized the "Stanfield anger" with his own dad and started working on minimizing it in himself. Then as I grew up, and before my grandfather passed, I saw some of it, and then I too worked to minimize it in my own life. That is one way that we have tried to work on our anger and remove that stigma from our name, but it is still a struggle sometimes. If we had not at least recognized it and had not started working on it in our lives, it might have grown into something monstrous, perhaps uncontrollable.

The first way to deal with anger is to recognize it in yourself. Recognize what triggers it inside of you and try not to ignore it and let it build up inside of you. Once you can pinpoint what triggers it, you can pray for God to remove those things from controlling your emotions. You can also sometimes distance yourself from certain situations that would put you around those triggers. Once these triggers have been identified, you have to search your heart and listen to what God tells you in regards to your anger. He may use anger to bring you to a place of seeking Him. I don't know how many times I have popped off with anger and will have everyone in my house upset with me, and I will find myself alone in a room wondering what just happened. I will feel completely stupid over the fight my temper just caused and embarrassed over how I just acted. Every single time I calm down, the first thing I feel is God's presence, and I always find myself asking Him for forgiveness and praying that He will help me fix the situation. I guess even as I type this, I realize that it is that tugging at my heart to seek God's forgiveness that is probably Him getting my attention for things other than just forgiveness.

I think in times like that, God is more interested in getting to the root of the anger and not just comforting me for acting like a fool in my anger. I think God wants us to empty out our hearts with junk like anger and fill our hearts with His grace and love. If we are right with God and fill our hearts with the right things, then we no longer have room for anger and things of this world that cause turmoil in our lives. Philippians 4:8 says, "Finally, brothers and sisters, whatever is pure, whatever is lovely, whatever is admirable—if anything is excellent or praiseworthy—think about such things."

So, when you find yourself sitting in a room by yourself feeling stupid after a dumb anger episode, seek the Lord and see what He really wants you to learn from the experience. Seek forgiveness from Him, but also seek forgiveness from those who had to witness your temper, even if you think someone else started it or played a role in it. The Bible says in Matthew 6:15, "But if you do not forgive others their sins, your Father will not forgive your sins." That is a pretty powerful statement. Our all-forgiving God actually has some things He just doesn't look past and forgive. This is one of them, so it is very important to not hold grudges against anyone in anger. You have to put your pride aside and ask for forgiveness and grow in your walk through it.

Once you can get to a place where you recognize your

anger, you also have to be able to keep it in check. One of the wisest verses on anger is James 1:19, "Everyone should be quick to listen, slow to speak and slow to become angry." What power over anger in those words! Think about how many fights or arguments or times you have been angry began by simply not listening to one another. That verse first says to "be quick to listen," meaning first take time to really listen to each other or be aware of the situation. Try to understand the other person's side of things and feelings. Then it says to be "slow to speak," meaning keep your mouth shut if you are only going to intensify the situation. Think about the old saying we have all heard that says, "Momma always said if you can't say something nice, don't say anything at all." I think most situations can be resolved if people are slow to speak when anger creeps in. Then, most importantly, the verse says to be "slow to become angry." Take that one to heart and go back to the point of keeping your heart filled with God's grace and love to the point that it is overflowing and people can sense it and feel it from you, and that in itself will help put out the fuse of anger.

Do not let Satan use anger in your life to control you, but rather control your anger and show Satan that he will lose that battle with you. The irony of it is that when we overcome our anger, Satan then gets angry and has to deal with it instead of us, and guess what: he has no one to help him deal with it like we do. Being slow to anger shows great strength and leadership. Having self-control will bring more blessings to your life and will bless those around you as well.

> *Refrain from anger and turn from wrath; do not fret—it leads only to evil.*
>
> **Psalm 37:8**
>
> *In your anger do not sin. Do not let the sun go down while you are still angry.*
>
> **Ephesians 4:26**
>
> *Get rid of all bitterness, rage and anger, brawling and slander, along with every form of malice.*
>
> **Ephesians 4:31**
>
> *A person's wisdom yields patience; it is to one's glory to overlook an offense.*
>
> **Proverbs 19:11**
>
> *Love is patient, love is kind. It does not envy, it does not boast, it is not proud. It does not dishonor others, it is not self-seeking, it is not easily angered, it keeps no record of wrongs.*
>
> **1 Corinthians 13:4–5**
>
> *Fools give full vent to their rage, but the wise bring calm in the end.*
>
> **Proverbs 29:11**
>
> *Do not be quickly provoked in your spirit, for anger resides in the lap of fools.*
>
> **Ecclesiastes 7:9**

Do not take revenge, my dear friends, but leave room for God's wrath, for it is written: 'It is mine to avenge; I will repay,' says the Lord.

Romans 12:19

Better a patient person than a warrior, one with self-control than one who takes a city.

Proverbs 16:32

Don't have anything to do with foolish and stupid arguments, because you know they produce quarrels. And the Lord's servant must not be quarrelsome but must be kind to everyone, able to teach, not resentful.

2 Timothy 2:23–24

Therefore, as God's chosen people, holy and dearly loved, clothe yourselves with compassion, kindness, humility, gentleness and patience. Bear with each other and forgive one another if any of you has a grievance against someone. Forgive as the Lord forgave you. And over all these virtues put on love, which binds them all together in perfect unity. Let the peace of Christ rule in your hearts, since as members of one body you were called to peace. And be thankful.

Colossians 3:12–15

PROFANE LANGUAGE

This is one of my personal struggles that I battle every single day. I work in construction, so I deal with a lot of things and situations where problems can arise, and anger can creep in, and before you know it, you find yourself yelling and cussing. This is one struggle that I think has gotten so typical of Hellven Christians that we don't even realize we do it half the time, or we do not care unless we are around certain people or at certain places. That is because Satan has whispered in the ear of Christians and said, "It's no big deal these days," and "Everyone does it, so don't even worry about it." It's become the official language of Hellven.

For some older readers, we can remember back twenty to thirty years ago to a time you would never hear cussing on TV or the radio. When songs came out with a lot of cussing in them, people would protest, and even our government got involved. You would not dare cuss around your parents or elders in fear of getting your head slapped off or a bar of soap in your mouth.

Nowadays, that's abuse. Nowadays, cussing is "freedom of speech," and profanity is just a normal way of speaking. Nowadays, TV shows and radios do not even bleep out the cuss words, and it is no longer frowned on. You can't listen to non-Christian music without hearing cuss words or profanity. I have two young daughters, and they like to link their phones up to my truck when we go somewhere so they can listen to "their" music. The next thing I know, I hear cuss words every other line. I remember one time saying, "Put on something that doesn't have cussing in it," and my daughter turned off her phone. I said, "Why did you do that?" She said, "Because I think all of my songs cuss, Dad." I thought to myself how pathetic that was and how disappointed I felt in myself for allowing my daughters to continually listen to that stuff and not bring them up better. The problem is that I'm a citizen of Hellven, and so are they.

Another thing that comes to my mind about profanity is how Satan has created clever ways to disguise profanity or to fool us all into thinking we aren't really using profanity when we actually are. One of the worst of these is us actually even breaking one of the commandments, which is saying the Lord's name in vain. You hear it daily in some form or another if you think about it. How many times a day do you hear or even say, "OMG"? If you are saying that, you are taking the Lord's name in vain and probably not even batting an eye over it. Just about every cuss word these days has a "clean" version, but you may as well be saying the real words because they all mean the same thing. Some of the slang words have made themselves into dictionaries, and they have even made a slang word dictionary that is very popular, called the "Urban Dictionary," which is filled with alternative cuss words and profanity. It's another example of how we all fail miserably at our walk with God.

I want to take a minute and share my own experiences on this struggle and see if you can relate. Here is how a typical day goes in regards to this struggle for me. I use my thirty-minute drive to work each day as a time of prayer and to listen to Christian music. My intention is to pray for my family and then pray for God to help me with my struggles. I think we all can identify our main struggles or sins. They are the ones we constantly sound like broken records during our prayers where we have to ask God for forgiveness for the same things daily. My language is one of them. When I pray each morning, I ask for forgiveness for my language, and I vow to do better that day. I even ask God to take that language from my vocabulary and use Scripture to say, "Do not let anything unwholesome come out of my mouth today." Then I finish my prayers with other things, turn up some Christian music, and by the time I get to my office, I feel like I just left a good service at church and am ready to conquer my day. This is right around 7:50 in the morning. I get to my desk and start checking emails, and my phone rings. It's a call from one of my superintendents at a job site who proceeds to tell me about some subcontractor that is causing problems or something that has gone wrong on the project. The next thing you know, he is cussing about it, and then I join right in. I get off the phone, and the conviction starts. I think, *Why did you do that, David?* I ask for forgiveness and go on about my day. Similar things continue to happen, and before you know it, I'm doing it, and the conviction doesn't follow. I don't even realize I'm doing it. Then I get home from work, and my wife gets on to me for it and tells me I really need to work on my language and to stop cussing all the time. All of a sudden, the conviction of the entire day comes rushing back in, and I ask for forgiveness again. These same steps start right back over the next morning. It is a continuous pattern of how I let this struggle rule me.

You know, the fact is that God does forgive me every single day that I ask Him to. He does take that language from my vocabulary, and He washes my mouth clean. It's me that is the problem. I fill my head so full of this language by listening to bad music, watching shows that are filled with it, surrounding myself with people who use it and accept it as normal, that it just goes out of control, at least for a citizen of Hellven like me.

Another thing that blows my mind about this struggle is how we can cut it completely off like a switch when we are around certain people or if we walk into a church. I know I can. I wouldn't dare cuss around my parents or for sure while I am in a church. The thought does not even cross my mind. How is that? How can I struggle with it all the time away from certain people or places but naturally turn it off in those situations? If you were raised in a Christian home or grew up in church, then I'm sure you can relate to this. If you are a new Christian or struggling with your faith, then you may not experience this type of natural guard against your language. I think that deep down, when we peel back the layers of trash that we let Hellven pile up in our hearts, there are just some basic values that hold true, and we know deep down that we shouldn't use bad language at all, but especially not in the house of God. Our hearts and spirit know it and take over because we relate God's house to the presence of God, and we would never talk like that in front of Him. Would we?

Well, Satan, who, by the way, rules Hellven, has got the last laugh on this one. He has all of us fooled into the old "out of sight, out of mind" concept. We walk out of that church or away from certain people, and it is like that switch goes back off, and here we go again, and we do not even realize that God is still there with us. Did you know that the Bible has at least eighteen verses that specifically talk about the omnipresence of God? Omnipresence means *He is everywhere at the same time*. That means when we leave the church or the presence of certain people who we would never cuss around, God is still there and still hears us. He sees all, hears all, and knows all.

To overcome this struggle, we first have to realize that there is no walking away from His presence and truly believe and understand this. We have to realize that we are ourselves the temple of God. The Bible says in

1 Corinthians 6:19, "Do you not know that your bodies are temples of the Holy Spirit, who is in you, whom you have received from God? You are not your own." Really think about that for a minute. This basically says that we, as Christians, are like a church building because God dwells in us. Just like when we cut off our language when we walk into church, we ought to do the same everywhere because we *are* the "church."

I think Satan and Hellven don't spend time concentrating on filling our heads with this language, but rather building blinders for Christians so that we do not wake up and see that God is with us at all times and not just in the church where we tend to leave Him. It's these blinders that really keep us from having freedom over this struggle.

I ask you to join with me and rip off the blinders and realize that God is with you always. I think if we can get that through our worldly heads, then we can let that natural defense from the foul language, which miraculously switches on when we walk into an actual church, be on at all times, no matter where we are or who we are with. That is the key to beating this struggle. If you really stop and think about it, that is the key to most of the struggles in our lives.

I challenge you to take the fact that the Lord is with you everywhere you go to the heart and dwell on Him throughout each day and see if you notice a difference in the language you use, how you act, your attitude, and who you choose to be. Pray that God will help you keep His presence known to you all throughout the day and that He will help tame your tongue.

All that said, taming the tongue is not an easy task, and it will be difficult, even as we set our sights on God. I want to start my verses for this chapter with a group of verses from James that talk about the difficulty of taming the tongue so you can see that God knows how hard this struggle is to overcome. As you read it, though, remember that God is going to help you along the way because He does not want you to battle this struggle alone.

> *We all stumble in many ways. Anyone who is never at fault in what they say is perfect, able to keep their whole body in check.*
> *When we put bits into the mouths of horses to make them obey us, we can turn the whole animal. Or take ships as an example. Although they are so large and are driven by strong winds, they are steered by a very small rudder wherever the pilot wants to go. Likewise, the tongue is a small part of the body, but it makes great boasts. Consider what a great forest is set on fire by a small spark. The tongue also is a fire, a world of evil among the parts of the body. It corrupts the whole body, sets the whole course of one's life on fire, and is itself set on fire by hell.*
> *All kinds of animals, birds, reptiles and sea creatures are being tamed and have been tamed by mankind, but no human being can*

tame the tongue. It is a restless evil, full of deadly poison.
With the tongue we praise our Lord and Father, and with it we curse human beings, who have been made in God's likeness. Out of the same mouth come praise and cursing. My brothers and sisters, this should not be.

James 3:2–10

Do not let any unwholesome talk come out of your mouths, but only what is helpful for building others up according to their needs, that it may benefit those who listen.

Ephesians 4:29

But now you must also rid yourselves of all such things as these: anger, rage, malice, slander, and filthy language from your lips. Do not lie to each other, since you have taken off your old self with its practices and have put on the new self, which is being renewed in knowledge in the image of its Creator.

Colossians 3:8–10

Nor should there be obscenity, foolish talk or coarse joking, which are out of place, but rather thanksgiving.

Ephesians 5:4

For by your words you will be acquitted, and by your words you will be condemned.

Matthew 12:37

Avoid godless chatter, because those who indulge in it will become more and more ungodly.

2 Timothy 2:16

You shall not misuse the name of the LORD your God, for the LORD will not hold anyone guiltless who misuses his name.

Exodus 20:7

For, 'Whoever would love life and see good days must keep their tongue from evil and their lips from deceitful speech.'

1 Peter 3:10

Those who guard their lips preserve their lives, but those who speak rashly will come to ruin.

Proverbs 13:3

Don't let anyone look down on you because you are young, but set an example for the believers in speech, in conduct, in love, in faith and in purity.

1 Timothy 4:12

WORRY

As a citizen of Hellven, Satan will constantly fill your head with worry. This is one of his weapons against us. He uses deceitfulness to help plant things in our thoughts. When Satan puts worry in your life, think of it as a drop of food coloring in a large glass of water. If you have seen that before, then you have seen what that tiny drop will do to the water. It starts as a dark spot of color that slowly creeps its way down into the glass, and then when it gets stirred up, it completely takes over the water and turns it into a solid color. It takes such little effort for Satan to simply squeeze a drop of worry into your life, and then he sits back and watches what you will let it do. It takes over your thoughts, creeps deeper into your life, then you stir things up over it, and before you know it, you have let it take over completely.

The worst part of worrying is that it leads to so many more problems and struggles once you stir it up and let it take over. Excessive worrying can lead to even worse problems in our lives, such as anxiety and stress, and it can even become a physical thing in your life. It can affect your health to the point that your body will react the same way it would react to physical danger or harm. You will also physically wear yourself out because you put your brain into constant focus on what you are worrying about. All of this can lead to more serious problems such as anxiety attacks, strokes, or heart attacks. Worrying can also affect your everyday life and ruin your relationships, your appetite, and your daily functionality. It's simply not healthy to worry.

In the US alone, anxiety disorders affect nearly forty million adults, and these are the people that actually admit they have a problem and take steps to get help. I bet excessive worrying and anxiety are struggles that we all face on a daily basis. I know I do. I am excessive with it. I constantly worry about my finances and making sure I am providing for my family adequately. Any time something small pops up on me that I wonder if I can overcome, I will just worry to death about it instead of giving it to God and asking Him to help me or provide for me. Even worse, I will bottle it up and not let anyone else even know I am worried about it, which makes it twice as hard to overcome.

Again, as a citizen of Hellven, it's our God blinders that we wear that cause us to not give our worries to the Lord. It's pretty simple, yet we simply do not do it. God tells us in His Word not to worry in some form or another at least 365 times. I would say that He is trying to get His point across. Sometimes we like to say, "Easier said than done," but God makes it easy if we will just take His word for it and let things go before God. He does not want us to have to carry the weight of worry and stress on our shoulders. Just like He takes away our sins and washes us clean, He will also take away your worries and anxiety if you let Him. Then you will feel the weight released. He also does not care what the worry is about, and nothing is too big or too small for our God. As a matter of fact, God promises to give us peace that passes all understanding when we give Him our burdens. He also promises rest once we give it to Him. Peace and rest can be a huge blessing to someone who spends all of their time worrying over things of this world. So if you find yourself worrying, first try giving it to God instead of dwelling on it and letting it control you. Also, let your loved ones know that you are struggling with the worry so that they can pray for you and help you through it. Do not hold it all in and make it grow.

There are other simple things that God equips us with that we can naturally do to help with worries and anxiety too. We can exercise, which produces chemicals in our bodies that help strengthen our immune system and makes us feel physically better. Being in better physical shape helps keep stress levels down and under control. We can also watch what we eat and drink and avoid too many stimulants such as caffeine which trigger jitters and the nervous feelings that come along with anxiety. God also equipped us with a powerful self-consciousness that we can use to recognize times when we become stressed and anxious, and we can remove ourselves from the situation or find a quiet place to talk to God and cast our worries on Him like He wants us to.

Once you can begin to give your worries to God, you will also need to find things to replace that worry with healthier alternatives. Change your attitude and decide that you want to live a worry-free life like God intends for you. You must make a decision to want to please God more than yourself, which in itself makes worrying about petty things seem ridiculous. Replace your worry with prayer and when it tries to creep back in, just ask God to take it away and have faith that He will handle it. Cast your cares on God and let Him know that you fully trust in Him and watch your worries disappear for good.

> *Do not be anxious about anything, but in every situation, by prayer and petition, with thanksgiving, present your requests to God. And the peace of God, which transcends all understanding, will guard your hearts and your minds in Christ Jesus.*
>
> **Philippians 4:6–7**

> *Therefore I tell you, do not worry about your life, what you will eat or drink; or about your body, what you will wear. Is not life more than food, and the body more than clothes?*
>
> **Matthew 6:25**

> *Cast all your anxiety on him because he cares for you.*
>
> **1 Peter 5:7**

But seek first his kingdom and his righteousness, and all these things will be given to you as well. Therefore do not worry about tomorrow, for tomorrow will worry about itself. Each day has enough trouble of its own.

Matthew 6:33–34

Come to me, all you who are weary and burdened, and I will give you rest. Take my yoke upon you and learn from me, for I am gentle and humble in heart, and you will find rest for your souls. For my yoke is easy and my burden is light.

Matthew 11:28–30

Peace I leave with you; my peace I give you. I do not give to you as the world gives. Do not let your hearts be troubled and do not be afraid.

John 14:27

And my God will meet all your needs according to the riches of his glory in Christ Jesus.

Philippians 4:19

Set your minds on things above, not on earthly things.

Colossians 3:2

But those who hope in the LORD will renew their strength. They will soar on wings like eagles; they will run and not grow weary, they will walk and not be faint.

Isaiah 40:31

The LORD himself goes before you and will be with you; he will never leave you nor forsake you. Do not be afraid; do not be discouraged.

Deuteronomy 31:8

RELATIONSHIPS

Relationships are a huge part of our lives, whether we are talking about our relationships with God, our family, our spouse, our friends, coworkers, or just those around us that we interact with every day. A relationship is "the way in which two or more people are connected and behave toward each other." It is a state of being connected in some form or fashion. Relationships can be good, or they can be bad, and they can definitely be a struggle.

Since we live in a world filled with problems, struggles, and warped views of how God intends our relationships to look, it makes it very difficult to have good ones. Look at key issues our world faces that have to do with relationships, such as divorce rates, bullying, criticism of each other, violence, and other things that stem from the way we treat each other. Divorce rates in the United States alone are currently at 40 to 50 percent, and when divorced people marry again, their divorce rates are even higher. These rates have been steadily climbing every year since the 1940s.

Almost one out of every four students in schools across our country report being bullied during the school year. On top of that, studies show that 64 percent of children who do get bullied do not even report it. Conflicts, fighting, and wars happen all around the world and are daily topics on the news. Mass shootings and violence have become common and frequent stories. Racial tensions have flared back up after our country had made good progress with it. I could go on and on with examples of what relationships look like here in Hellven. Satan runs rampant in our relationships, and it is more obvious now than ever; with these things happening all around us, it's no wonder that we struggle to know what our relationships should look like these days.

I also believe that all types of relationship struggles stem from the behavior of human beings and how we treat each other. I think you can take it a step further and say that most of the problems in the world today are caused by the behaviors of people. Really think about these for a minute.

- Bullying is defined as the act of using force or intimidation to get someone else to do something against their will. It can be teasing, name-calling, taunting, causing physical and emotional harm, spreading rumors, or embarrassing someone.
- The top reasons that marriages and dating relationships end are infidelity, emotional and/or

physical abuse, communication problems and/or arguing.

- Worldly conflicts and wars arise because of changing relationships between countries or governments. Countries will go halfway across the world to involve themselves in the affairs of other countries when they see behaviors they feel are out of control.

- Environmental issues we face are even caused by the behavior of humans and the impact we have on the planet.

It's all behavioral, it's all relative, and it all destroys relationships. So how do we fix it? How are we supposed to work on our relationships when we are surrounded by so many poor examples and problems? The answers are easier said than done in the sinful Hellven world we live in, and I am certainly not a relationship expert. I fail at my personal relationships daily and let those around me down often because it has become our nature to fail. I do know where to look for guidance on them, however.

As Christians, we are lucky enough to have the best resource available on relationships, which is the Bible. It is filled with examples of great relationships and what God intends our relationships to be like. First and foremost, it shows us what our relationship with God is supposed to be and how to put that relationship first. It shows us how to prioritize our relationships and how to treat others. It shows us how important relationships are to God and how He wants us to have good relationships in our lives.

I believe that the key to all relationships is how we prioritize them. If we put God first in all we do and make our relationship with Him the most important one we have, then we automatically strengthen all other relationships in our lives. When thinking about this, I am reminded of an old illustration that I first heard in a young married couple's Sunday school class that my wife and I attended as newlyweds. I have since seen the illustration multiple times and have also seen it in other Christian books, but I want to share it here with you.

Look at the triangle illustration below. Imagine any of the people in your life, whether it be a spouse, your child, a friend, a coworker, or even an enemy, and plug them into the "others" spot on the diagram. If you and that person are trying to work on your relationship together, it has to start by working on each of your relationships with God. When each of you begins to get closer to God, amazingly, you will automatically become closer in your relationship with the other person.

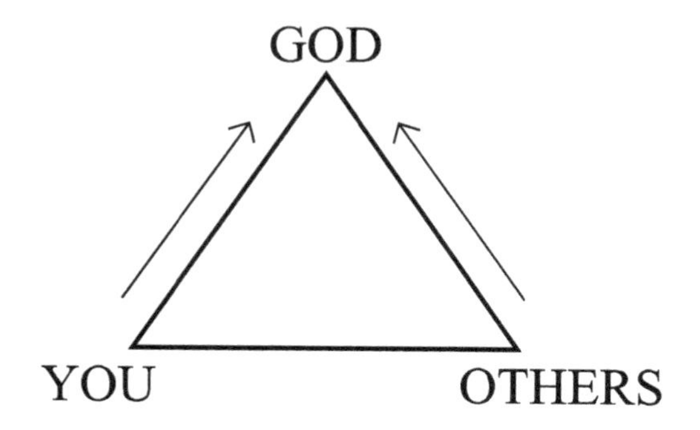

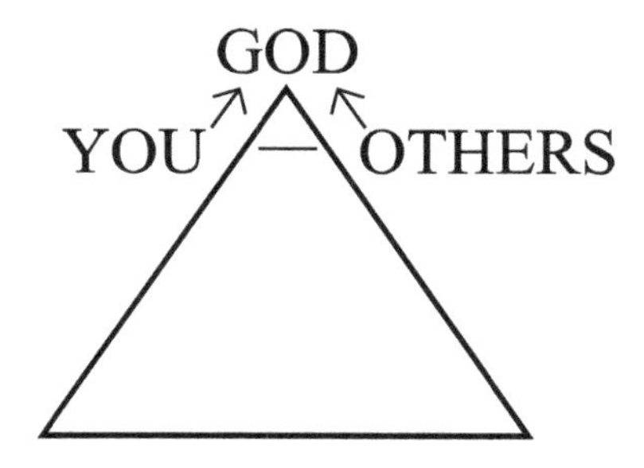

You can only control your own relationship with God, however. You can do all the right things and put Him first in your life, but that does not mean that "others" will always do the same. You may reach the top of the triangle sometimes, and the "others" are still distant from you. They are still at the bottom because they do not seek that relationship with God first. If you find yourself there, all you can do is pray for them and concentrate on continually strengthening your relationship with God. I can promise you that God will answer your prayers one way or another. If it is His will for you to have a relationship with the other person, He will get that person focused on Him, and they will meet you there at the top, and it will be the best relationship you could imagine. If it is a relationship that God knows is not healthy for you or not in His will, then by having that strong relationship with God, He will clearly show you and help release that relationship from your life.

So, as hard as it is, especially in the world we live in now, if you want to have good relationships, healthy relationships, loving relationships, then seek God first and build a strong relationship with Him. Pray for God to put that same burden on the heart of the other person or people in your life. Just like the triangle depicts, it is often an uphill battle, but the rewards are greater than the struggles.

> *'Teacher, which is the greatest commandment in the Law?' Jesus replied: 'Love the Lord your God with all your heart and with all your soul and with all your mind.' This is the first and greatest commandment. And the second is like it: 'Love your neighbor as yourself.'*
>
> **Matthew 22:36–39**

> *Be completely humble and gentle; be patient, bearing with one another in love. Make every effort to keep the unity of the Spirit through the bond of peace.*
>
> **Ephesians 4:2–3**

> *One who has unreliable friends soon comes to ruin, but there is a friend who sticks closer than a brother.*
>
> **Proverbs 18:24**

> *'The man who hates and divorces his wife,' says the LORD, the God of Israel, 'does violence to the one he should protect,' says the LORD Almighty. So be on your guard, and do not be unfaithful.*
>
> **Malachi 2:16**

> *Love is patient, love is kind. It does not envy, it does not boast, it is not proud. It does not*

dishonor others, it is not self-seeking, it is not easily angered, it keeps no record of wrongs. Love does not delight in evil but rejoices with the truth. It always protects, always trusts, always hopes, always perseveres.

1 Corinthians 13:4–7

A new command I give you: Love one another. As I have loved you, so you must love one another. By this everyone will know that you are my disciples, if you love one another.

John 13:34–35

Live in harmony with one another. Do not be proud, but be willing to associate with people of low position. Do not be conceited. Do not repay anyone evil for evil. Be careful to do what is right in the eyes of everyone. If it is possible, as far as it depends on you, live at peace with everyone. Do not take revenge, my dear friends, but leave room for God's wrath, for it is written: 'It is mine to avenge; I will repay,' says the Lord. On the contrary: 'If your enemy is hungry, feed him; if he is thirsty, give him something to drink. In doing this, you will heap burning coals on his head.' Do not be overcome by evil, but overcome evil with good.

Romans 12:16–21

Be kind and compassionate to one another, forgiving each other, just as in Christ God forgave you.

Ephesians 4:32

But seek first his kingdom and his righteousness, and all these things will be given to you as well.

Matthew 6:33

Above all, love each other deeply, because love covers over a multitude of sins. Offer hospitality to one another without grumbling.

1 Peter 4:8–9

Do not worship any other god, for the LORD, whose name is Jealous, is a jealous God.

Exodus 34:14

FORGIVENESS

Before I dive into forgiveness, I just want to throw in another quick reference to something else neat that just happened to confirm that I am on track with following God's direction for me in regards to this book. Some may think it is coincidence, but I know it is obedience.

I got up early just a few minutes ago, just like I have done to write some before I start my day. I took a look at where I am in my progress, and I saw that I was at this "Forgiveness" chapter. I then pulled up Pandora on my computer and turned on some worship music, which I also always do while writing. The very first song that came on was called "Forgiveness" by Matthew West. I had never heard it, so I just sat there and listened to the whole song, which got my mind focused on the topic. I thought it was awesome since thirty minutes before, I was lying in bed trying to convince myself that it would be okay to skip writing this morning and just be lazy. I'm glad I got up and am sitting here writing. Now let's see what God has to tell us about forgiveness.

Forgiveness is a hard pill for us Hellven citizens to swallow. We preach it, we teach it, we are taught forgiveness all of our lives, but when it comes time to forgive others for wrongs, we can't seem to do it. Struggling with forgiveness can destroy relationships; it can rip families apart; it can turn your soul bitter.

Think about this. Our main Christian beliefs are built around the fact that God sent His Son, Jesus, to die for us so He could *forgive* us of our sins and wash us clean. That is God's greatest gift to us. How much joy do you think it gives Satan to see us not return the favor and be un-forgiving to each other? I would imagine that un-forgiveness has to be one of Satan's favorite things. On the flip side of that, think about what a slap in the face it is to God when He sees us being unforgiving. It has to hurt knowing what He did for us.

Most of the things we all have trouble forgiving people for these days are petty if you stop and think about it. I've seen lifelong friends stop talking to each other because one friend referred to a third person as their "best friend" instead of that friend. They both know it is petty and just a term or title, yet they still don't talk to each other or see each other anymore. The distancing of themselves and the ignoring of each other has only pushed them further apart and made it even harder to forgive each other for the pettiness and move forward as friends again. All it would take is for one of them to initiate a move, ask for forgiveness, and forget about it. Those two words, "forgive me," are all that keep their friendship from existing anymore.

Other things in our lives may be deeper and harder to just forgive and forget. Since losing our son, my wife and I have had people in our lives that have either said things that were insensitive, acted insensitively, or just been vacant to us while dealing with our grief. Some of them are very close friends, and some of them are family. We have to constantly tell ourselves that they do not know how to act around us or handle our situation because they have not been in our shoes before. Telling yourself these things over and over does not make you want to forgive them for what you feel are wrongs, though. We often have talks about some of them and find ourselves wanting to call them up and let them have a piece of our minds and make sure they know how they have hurt us, hurt our kids, or just put them in their place. We feel like we are entitled to an apology and that it would make us feel a little better knowing we hurt them right back.

The truth is, these people may not even realize they have done anything to hurt us. They may feel so scared to say or do the wrong things around us that they choose to not say anything to us or come around us anymore because they don't want to cause more pain for us. They may not realize that simply being there for us and saying they are thinking about us is enough. They may not realize that some things they have said or done were taken the wrong way or hurt our feelings. They may have had the best intentions in the world, and we just had different opinions of it, yet here we are, feeling angry and hurt over it and not forgiving them.

In a perfect world, we would be able to tell them how we feel, they would apologize and ask for forgiveness, and we would all move forward as if nothing ever happened.

That is the way God intends it to be, yet we cannot seem to find a way to tell them how we feel without hurting their feelings; they take things the wrong way and get angry; a wedge gets built; no one forgives, and the entire situation gets worse. That is the perfect example of how Satan wants to see us deal with things.

It is so easy to get caught in this trap. It is more comfortable and easier to be caught than it is to forgive and forget. Sometimes you just don't have the energy and would just rather ignore the problem than deal with it. It all goes together and will wear you out even more. I'm living in this trap myself right now, and it is definitely a struggle.

There can also be situations in some of our lives that we will automatically consider unforgivable. Maybe things such as being physically or mentally harmed or abused. Maybe you have a friend or family member that was killed by someone else, accidentally or intentionally. How do we forgive people that have done these types of things? I do not have an example of this personally, but if I try to imagine forgiving someone if they killed one of my family members, I have a hard time thinking I could ever do it.

I believe that forgiving people who have hurt us or wronged us is one of the hardest things that God asks us to do, but it parallels the hardest thing God has ever had to do, which was to watch His own Son die for our sins, for our forgiveness. I think this is exactly what God wants us to think about when considering our forgiveness for others. He wants to be our example. He wants Jesus to be our example. In order for any of us to be forgiven of our sins and have eternal life in heaven, Jesus had to die and take the punishment for our sins. He hung on a cross and not only went through the physical torture leading up to and on the cross, but He also went through the emotional torture of having the sins of the world dumped on Him. He went to hell and back for you and me. While He hung there barely clinging onto His life on earth and feeling the torments of hell, you would think He would be like we are and want to curse the ones who put Him there that were gathered around mocking Him. You would think He would want nothing more than to strike them all down in revenge, which He did have the power to do. He could have just said the words, and He could have stopped His pain and torture. He could have chosen to not take on our sins for us. Instead, He called out to God, saying, "Father, Father, forgive them! They do not know what they are doing!" He asked for forgiveness for them, for us, and He took the punishment for us all. He set the ultimate example of forgiveness for us. We are lucky enough to not have to go through the physical torture part of that example, yet we put ourselves through the mental torture of holding grudges and living with the un-forgiveness.

Even with such a great example, it's still a lot easier said than done to truly forgive someone that has hurt you, but not doing it can cause even more problems for you. Holding the hurt inside can change you completely. It can turn you into a bitter person, and it can become unhealthy for you. It can turn into anger, and before you know it, you are hurting others yourself, and it becomes a cycle, which is exactly what Satan wants. Also, how do we ask God to forgive us of our sins, yet we can't forgive others of theirs? Apparently pretty easily in our Hellven minds.

So, what can we do to get over ourselves and release our forgiveness? I think we have to first realize that forgiving someone of a wrong doesn't mean that we have to disregard the wrong. All forgiveness really has to mean is that you are no longer going to let the wrong someone does to you control you. You are no longer going to hold the grudge or disappointment inside and let it change you. You are simply releasing it. I think it is important to point out that in the Bible, the Greek translation of the word "forgiveness" means "to let go." God wants us to just let go of things and give them to Him. That's why He went through everything for us so that we wouldn't have to put ourselves through the hurt of dealing with things on our own.

Next, we all need to remember that none of us are perfect and that we all sin daily. We all constantly do things that we probably regret and that hurt others. None of us are exactly the same either, which means something that really hurts your feelings may not have the same effect on others. So we have to try to be aware of other people's feelings and try to understand their side of things as well as yours. Remember times in your life when you have done wrong and how good it felt to get forgiveness from someone you hurt, and then pass that same feeling along by forgiving someone who hurt you. Forgiveness is a give-and-take action, not a selfish action. It's just like your walk with God; it can't be a one-way street. You can't just constantly live in your sin and ask for forgiveness over and over without putting some effort into your relationship with God and giving back to Him. Likewise, you can't ask for forgiveness from others if you constantly don't forgive others yourself.

Lastly, but most importantly, we need to be quick in our forgiveness. Just like all of our worldly, Hellven struggles, when we don't forgive and hold it in, it starts to smolder inside of us. It starts to spread into anger, resentment, hate, and it spreads all over us like a wildfire. Before you know it, you are consumed with it, and it takes you over. Even if it started as something small or petty, it will take control of you, and you will turn it into something major because it will control your attitude, and you will start to return the wrong back onto the person that wronged you. It will become a cycle of wrongs back and forth between you and the original person, and then the fire will spread to other people around each of you. You will spread it to those close to you, who will, in turn, create anger and hatred towards the other person and vice-versa. Now instead of just two people being hurt or upset with each other, there are several people upset and hurt, all because the original two people could not forgive and put the small flame out before it spread. This happens every day around us. We have to squash things before the fire in and around us can get started. You can't control the other person's actions, but you can at least take a stand yourself and refuse Satan the chance to stir things up even more by letting things smolder inside yourself and fuel the fire. Even when you don't get a response from the other person, forgive them and let go. Even if that means that person will no longer be a part of your life, forgive them and let them go. Sometimes God just wants to see the obedience in you to release blessings on you.

> *For if you forgive other people when they sin against you, your heavenly Father will also forgive you. But if you do not forgive others their sins, your Father will not forgive your sins.*
>
> **Matthew 6:14–15**

> *Get rid of all bitterness, rage and anger, brawling and slander, along with every form of malice. Be kind and compassionate to one another, forgiving each other, just as in Christ God forgave you.*
>
> **Ephesians 4:31–32**

Therefore confess your sins to each other and pray for each other so that you may be healed. The prayer of a righteous person is powerful and effective.

James 5:16

So watch yourselves. 'If your brother or sister sins against you, rebuke them; and if they repent, forgive them. Even if they sin against you seven times in a day and seven times come back to you saying 'I repent,' you must forgive them.'

Luke 17:3–4

Then Peter came to Jesus and asked, 'Lord, how many times shall I forgive my brother or sister who sins against me? Up to seven times?' Jesus answered, 'I tell you, not seven times, but seventy-seven times.'

Matthew 18:21–22

Do not repay anyone evil for evil. Be careful to do what is right in the eyes of everyone. Do not take revenge, my dear friends, but leave room for God's wrath, for it is written: 'It is mine to avenge; I will repay,' says the Lord. On the contrary: 'If your enemy is hungry, feed him; if he is thirsty, give him something to drink.'

Romans 12:17, 19–20

Therefore, as God's chosen people, holy and dearly loved, clothe yourselves with compassion, kindness, humility, gentleness and patience. Bear with each other and forgive one another if any of you has a grievance against someone. Forgive as the Lord forgave you.

Colossians 3:12–13

Therefore I tell you, whatever you ask for in prayer, believe that you have received it, and it will be yours. And when you stand praying, if you hold anything against anyone, forgive them, so that your Father in heaven may forgive you your sins.

Mark 11:24–25

Do not judge, and you will not be judged. Do not condemn, and you will not be condemned. Forgive, and you will be forgiven.

Luke 6:37

If anyone has caused grief, he has not so much grieved me as he has grieved all of you to some extent—not to put it too severely. The punishment inflicted on him by the majority is sufficient. Now instead, you ought to forgive and comfort him, so that he will not be overwhelmed by excessive sorrow. I urge you, therefore, to reaffirm your love for him. Another reason I wrote you was to see if you would stand the test and be obedient in everything. Anyone you forgive, I also forgive. I have forgiven in the sight of Christ for your sake, in order that Satan might not outwit us.

Forgiveness

For we are not unaware of his schemes.

2 Corinthians 2:5–11

FINANCES

I looked up some financial figures for the average American adult, and I was not surprised by what I found. I saw that over seventy-six million of us are living paycheck to paycheck and barely getting by. That is a little over 31 percent of all adults in the US. I also found that over 41 percent of families that have an unexpected or emergency costing $400 could not even cover it and would have to borrow or sell something in order to pay it. About one-third of the US does not have any savings set aside for retirement either. This is all alarming, but what's even more alarming about it is that wages are at an all-time high, and a large percentage of these people struggling are even reporting six-digit incomes.

It sounds like a lot of us are struggling financially. Personally, I fit into this category of people. I want to share some stories of my career and my finances with you, as this is what's on my heart for this chapter. My finances have been a roller coaster all of my adult life. I have had times when I couldn't make it to my next check and had things like cable, water, phone service, and even electricity cut off on some occasions over the years. I have had those unexpected bills or emergencies hit where I could not cover them and had to ask for advances in my pay or sell things. I actually had that happen as recently as a couple of weeks ago when we had our pet dog get sick and had an unexpected vet trip.

At one point in my career, I owned my own business and ended up doing pretty well with it and made the most money of my career. During that time, I spoiled my wife and kids and basically never said no. We sold our house that we had been in for several years and upgraded to a brand new custom-built house. My wife and I each had brand new vehicles, and I also went out and bought myself a jeep just to go mudding in because I always wanted one. My wife was able to quit working during this time also and enjoy time raising our kids at home. We were living the dream, and it was a great time for us. The one thing I wasn't doing during that time, though, was tithing and putting God first in my finances that He was blessing me with. Then, around 2008, the economy got terrible, and everything changed. I quickly found my business running out of work, and it was a struggle just to keep my employees busy. I began having to let people go. I downsized the office and eventually moved my office into my house. I hung on to two employees who were my good friends as long as I could until I was actually paying them instead of bills. This just continued to spiral out of control until I was drowning in debt. It happened so quickly, and I had no choice but to file for bankruptcy. Before I knew it, I started losing everything. We lost all three vehicles and had to surrender our beautiful home. So in a blink of an eye, we had no home, no vehicle, and no work.

Even in one of the worst financial disasters of my life, God was still in control, and He had a plan for me. I had to begin reaching out to some of my business clients to see if anyone could offer me a job working directly for them. I quickly had two job offers. Both of them were literally half of what I had been making before my business crashed. Both of them also would force me to pack up my family and move out of the town we had lived in for over ten years and where we had started our family, which only made things sting worse for my wife and kids. One of my offers came from a strong Christian man in Shreveport, Louisiana, who I had been doing work for with my business for that past year or so. When I first reached out to him asking for a job, he wasn't even looking for a full-time employee, but he told me that God wanted him to think about it and that he would be in touch. It turned out that he and his business partner, his brother, had just had a big conversation about the future of their company and the need to find someone to help grow the company. They had actually started praying for God to show them what direction they needed to go and what to do, and I literally called him a few days later. It's hard to describe now, but the three of us immediately felt God's move in the situation, and we all knew that it was meant to be. When the salary was discussed, I put out a figure that was way out of their ballpark, and they countered with a number that I didn't think I could make ends meet with. I had to fully surrender to it, though, and trust that God would take care of my family and me and provide exactly what we needed, so we moved and started over. I was able to buy a truck from my dad, and we slowly started getting back on our feet.

I worked with that company for about four years and quickly moved up the ladder there and was continually blessed with raises at just the right time, but guess what, I still wasn't putting God first with our finances. I just never could figure out how I could give 10 percent of what was already so little in our tight budget. So, even though we were back on our feet and stable, we were still always living paycheck to paycheck. I ended up starting to do some work on the side to help us be a little more comfortable. As the side work increased, I took some focus off of my day job and what God had blessed me with there. One morning I got up early to go to work and was surprised to see that my boss had beat me to the office, which was strange. I walked in the office door, and he called me into his office and fired me on the spot. That was the second time in my life that I felt like I had lost everything financially. I was shocked and scared to death again, just like when my business went under. To this day, I still don't agree with anything he said or did that day, but I feel like whatever the Lord put on his heart was just part of God's plan for me, and even though it took me a long time to get over that one, I know now that it had to happen and I am actually thankful for it now.

I ended up without a job for about a month, but God gave me some odds and end work to get us by, and I was hired by another company where we lived, making right around what I was making. I quickly hit the ground running there with a new focus and commitment to my work. In a short time, I ended up being a company board member and took over an entire department of the company. God continued to bless me and provide for my family, even when I still didn't deserve it. During that next year, we were able to build a brand new home and were able to build it big enough to move my in-laws into it with us. It was perfect, and we all had our own space, and everything was great.

Shortly after getting settled in our nice new home, I began feeling like God still had something bigger for me and my career. I began feeling miserable with my job. It wasn't really what I enjoyed doing or something I could see myself doing for the rest of my career, and my boss pretty much told me I was topped out on his pay scale, which was depressing as I still was spinning my wheels right around the same spot for the past five years at that time. I began looking for job opportunities around the area, and there were plenty, but there was never anything that would pay me more than what I was making, and when I talked to people, they would tell me I was topped out for that area. So, I just kept on working the same job that I didn't really like and getting more depressed, all while my family was loving things and enjoying the new house.

I just couldn't shake off the feeling like God had more for me out there somewhere, so I ended up secretly looking at job opportunities elsewhere and was feeling like the Lord wanted me to look in the Dallas, Texas, area. I quickly found that there were a lot of jobs right up my alley there for pay that was a considerable step up for me. Before I could actually take the next step and apply to some, I had to break the news to my wife and see how she would take the news that I was miserable and wanted to move and leave our brand new house and uproot our kids again. Surprisingly, she was fully on board and supported me 100 percent. She thought I was crazy but wanted me to be happy and follow God's calling, so I started applying. The first day, I applied to around fifteen jobs, and within a week, I had three interviews set up. I set them up so that I could make the three-hour drive over to Dallas and have the first interview early in the day, another one close to lunchtime, and the last one mid-afternoon, and still get home at a decent time. By the end of the day, I had job offers from all three companies that I interviewed with and drove home to give my family and extended family the news that it looked like we would be moving. Luckily, I have an awesome wife and in-laws, and everyone was on board without any doubts. I simply listened to God, and He provided and blessed us for following Him.

The job I picked was my second interview. I somehow

knew it was the one when I walked into the place, even though it was the most awkward interview I had ever been on, and I thought I bombed it right off the bat. The owner interviewed me and basically told me I was not experienced enough, and I thought he didn't like me at all. The next thing I knew, he was telling me how he didn't even want to interview anyone from out of town, but that something drew him to my resume and that he felt that God had told him to take a chance on me. So, within ten minutes of walking in the door, I was being offered the job, and it was a substantial raise from what I had been making. My family and I got moved over soon after that, and within six months, I had doubled my salary from where I was in Shreveport, and I was loving my new job like no job I had ever done. After working there for a little over two years, my boss started talking to me about how he felt that God brought me to his business for a reason, and I shared with him that I felt the same way. I then got asked to be the vice president of the company. I have since moved on from there to other opportunities and have tried to continue to follow God's lead with my career, and He has always been faithful to provide for my family and me.

I look back on everything that has happened through my career since losing my business and everything basically, and I can clearly see the perfect path that God laid out for me. Every experience and job I had in between then and now gave me the exact tools and knowledge that allowed me to be successful with my current job. I am just in awe of what God has done to bring my family and me out of the scariest times financially. He is faithful even when we don't deserve one penny.

I'd like to tell you that after that happy-sounding ending, we never struggle with our finances now, but even though we are back to being comfortable, we still aren't getting ahead because I still am struggling with fully surrendering my tithes to God. I give with every check I get, but it's what I think I can give and not the full 10 percent that I am supposed to. I can sit here and admit that I am causing myself not to have the full blessings of God to be released by not doing it, but it's still hard to make that commitment and actually do it. I have been struggling with the fact that I help others and do some other things that I consider part of my tithe each month and that when I add it all up, it equals the 10 percent. I was moving right along thinking that until I recently heard a great message on Sunday from my pastor about tithing, and he showed us in God's Word where that 10 percent belongs directly to God and needs to come to His house, not anywhere else. I now realize that even though I have been blessed, I need to make that full commitment and bring my tithes directly to God in order to be fully blessed. I am convinced that true peace and happiness with your finances only comes when you are obedient in giving God that first 10 percent and having faith that He will provide for everything else. Now, if it were simple and easy, we would all be doing it, and we would probably see the most thriving economy ever seen, but obviously, it is a struggle in our current world because we aren't obedient with our finances.

I want to make it clear that being obedient in your giving is the number one way to help your finances, but I also do want to mention a few other things that can help you overcome your financial problems. First, just simply have faith that God will provide and take care of you. Even in your most stressful of situations with your finances, if you will just give it to God and ask Him to help you, He will. Lift your finances up to Him daily in prayer. Ask God to provide for your needs and to bless you financially, but at the same time, be thankful and express your gratitude to Him for all He does and provides for you. God wants to bless you and not only give you the means to get by but to provide in abundance for you. Just trust in Him. Secondly, be proactive in your situation. God wants you to have faith that He will provide, but just sitting there depressed about your situation and doing nothing to help will get you nowhere. Part of having faith is getting active, searching for things you can do to earn extra money, things you could possibly sell, and just getting out and asking God to lead you. By doing these things, you are showing God that you will follow Him, and He will recognize that and direct you to the right places or the right people that can be exactly what you need to receive His blessings.

So pray about your finances daily, have faith that God will provide, be thankful when He does, be proactive, and seek His direction and guidance. If you do these few things and give God back His firsts, His tithe, then there is no limit to what blessings He can pour out into your life. He is ready to bless you; just be faithful and obedient.

> *Do not be anxious about anything, but in every situation, by prayer and petition, with thanksgiving, present your requests to God.*
>
> **Philippians 4:6**
>
> *'Bring the whole tithe into the storehouse, that there may be food in my house. Test me in this,' says the LORD Almighty, 'and see if I will not throw open the floodgates of heaven and pour out so much blessing that there will not be room enough to store it.'*
>
> **Malachi 3:10**
>
> *Keep your lives free from the love of money and be content with what you have, because God has said, 'Never will I leave you; never will I forsake you.'*
>
> **Hebrews 13:5**
>
> *Those who want to get rich fall into temptation and a trap and into many foolish and harmful desires that plunge people into ruin and destruction. For the love of money is a root of all kinds of evil. Some people, eager for money, have wandered from the faith and pierced themselves with many griefs.*
>
> **1 Timothy 6:9–10**

'For I know the plans I have for you,' declares the LORD, 'plans to prosper you and not to harm you, plans to give you hope and a future.

Jeremiah 29:11

Ask and it will be given to you; seek and you will find; knock and the door will be opened to you. For everyone who asks receives; the one who seeks finds; and to the one who knocks, the door will be opened.

Matthew 7:7–8

Give, and it will be given to you. A good measure, pressed down, shaken together and running over, will be poured into your lap. For with the measure you use, it will be measured to you.

Luke 6:38

And my God will meet all your needs according to the riches of his glory in Christ Jesus.

Philippians 4:19

The wise store up choice food and olive oil, but fools gulp theirs down.

Proverbs 21:20

Remember this: Whoever sows sparingly will also reap sparingly, and whoever sows generously will also reap generously. Each of you should give what you have decided in your heart to give, not reluctantly or under compulsion, for God loves a cheerful giver. And God is able to bless you abundantly, so that in all things at all times, having all that you need, you will abound in every good work.

2 Corinthians 9:6–8

LIFE BALANCE

In the world we live in these days, there is more going on in the typical person's life than ever before. We all have so many struggles, issues with finances, issues with relationships, and all of the other things we have already talked about. We all constantly have things we are trying to fix or work on. How do we balance our time? How do we get everything done that we need to do? How do we please everyone and still have time for ourselves, or most importantly, for God?

This has become a big struggle for me for sure. I am the guy that feels like I have to be the provider and fix everything. It's just my personality, and it's who I am. I can't change it, or I wouldn't be who I am, but with that comes a lot of things I have to juggle. I'm a husband, a father, an employee, a boss, a provider, a comforter, and I wear many other hats. I'm typically up at 5:30 to 6:00 a.m. every day and don't slow down till bedtime each night. My whole career, I have constantly tried to better myself and better my situation for my family. I have just about always worked a full-time job and also done extra work on the side, getting up extra early or working late into the evening trying to earn extra money for my family. As I have moved up the ladder in my career, my day jobs have gotten more and more demanding of my time. As my kids have grown, they have gotten more demanding of my time. Life, in general, has just gotten more and more demanding and draining on me. Everything that has been thrown my way and my family's way just weighs down on top of everything else, and sometimes I seem to think I'm drowning. I often wonder how to balance everything, and sometimes it seems impossible, and when it gets that way, it's easy to make an excuse to not have time for God or church. Who's been there or can relate? Probably all of us.

Sometimes it's easy to get caught up in everything you have going on in your career, or just life in general, to start neglecting the things, or people in your life, or God. I believe while God is blessing your career and giving you new responsibilities, Satan's counteraction is to keep your focus fully on the responsibilities and blind you to the other things in your life. I think you can even be taking off in your career and thanking God the entire time for blessing your job and not even realizing you are neglecting other things or the people in your life. That is exactly what Satan wants too. Sometimes when things seem to be going really good for your career is when you really have to pray for protection from the enemy even more.

I know for myself, after moving into leadership and management roles in my career, it has brought a lot more responsibilities with it. I feel like I'm working about two and a half full-time jobs in one. I am busier than I have ever been with my work, yet I'm happier in my career than I have ever been. I find myself being consumed by it. I wake up in the middle of the night thinking about what I need to get done the next day or how to resolve some issue going on with one of my projects. I find myself talking to my wife about nothing but work when we are together. She has to tell me sometimes that she loves me but that she is sick of just talking about my work, and I have to snap out of it. On the one hand, it's great to do something you love for a living and enjoy it so much, but you also have to be able to balance it.

Jobs and careers can be one of the biggest things to balance your time with, but the daily things that life in general throws into the mix can often really stir things up. If you have kids, there can be homework, projects, sports games and practices, school programs, or a hundred other things that they always seem to have to go on. Or, your kids could just want to spend time with you and demand some of your time. Sometimes I would come home from a busy, hectic day at work and will just be physically and mentally drained, and I will just want to lie out on the couch and not do anything but relax. Then one of my kids will need me to take them to the store or will want to go do something. When they were a little younger, my kids would want me to play games or spend time with them. I know many times I would reject them, and they would tell me things like, "You are no fun anymore, Dad," or ask me why I don't spend more time with them. Thinking about it now, I am disappointed in myself for it, and I try to do better with it now, but it is hard sometimes. You end up realizing it when it's too late, and your kids grow to the point where it really is no fun hanging out with their parents, and you just miss out. Your spouse will also need your time, and making that time should also be a priority. One of the biggest reasons for the high divorce rates that we have right now is that couples don't spend quality time together. One of the two decides that other things in life are more important than their relationship with their spouse or kids, and those relationships crumble. Marriages come with enough challenges on their own and don't need to become even harder by one of the two people not putting in the time to strengthen the relationship. You have to make time for family.

The most important thing to make time in your life for, though, is to make time for God. Make time to spend with Him in prayer daily, even if it is a few minutes. I try to make sure to start every day with a prayer. I often say just about the same prayer: I just thank God for the new day and to be with my family and me as we go through the day. Even though it sounds like a broken record to me, God honors it and knows the desires of my heart. I also try to pray with my wife for this morning prayer when we are both up in the mornings, and it is even better that way. You can also do a quick daily devotional or read a passage of Scripture to start your day. Anything to just give God the first part of your day and to get a godly mindset will just start your day off on the right foot. I can tell you personally that as crazy and hectic as my life can get, I do know one thing to be true, that God has been there for me, even when I'm not making time for Him. Even when I don't deserve the help He gives me. Even when I flat out know I am disappointing Him. He's always there, and that never changes. You or I may distance ourselves from God by never making time for Him, but He is not the one that moved; we are.

We also need to make time to be in God's house every week and get involved with church. We are like vehicles that run all week with our busy lives, and we run out of gas by the end of the week. Think of church as your spiritual gas station. We need to be refilled with God's Word and hear what He is speaking through our pastors each week. We need to be rejuvenated with praise and worship weekly. We need all of these things, yet we don't make the time for them. We don't make the time for God. Statistics show that church attendance rates drop every year, which is funny because we seem to have more and more churches popping up every year. We are trying to create "new" church experiences and build bigger, better churches that look "cool." We are trying everything we can to make church an entertaining experience to draw more people in, but it shouldn't take that much work. We should just simply be making the time to be there, no matter where that is or what kind of building it is in.

In order to give some structure to all of the things we deal with every day, I want to mention a little saying that I'm sure most of us have heard at some point, but it is a simple thing to remember and try to follow. The saying is "Faith, family, and friends." This little saying puts everything into perspective for prioritizing your life. Your faith should always be first. The faith category is that time you give to God. Make it your number one priority, and everything else in your life will fall into place. Secondly is family. Put aside time for your family and spend quality time together, no matter how busy you are. Even when you think you absolutely don't have time, a few minutes with your spouse or children can make a huge difference in your relationships. Lastly is friends. Surround yourself with godly friends that you can also lean on for support and spend time doing things you enjoy. We all get so busy sometimes that we neglect our friendships, and it is important to keep our bonds with friends strong and let our friends know that we are still there, even when we are super busy. All of the other categories in our lives, such as work and hobbies, and on and on, will fall right in line where they are meant to be if we keep these few things in their places. Make God the number one priority in your life, and watch how He will bless your other relationships, your finances, your career, and all that you do. Slow down and be thankful for all that you do have and the blessings in your life.

But seek first his kingdom and his

righteousness, and all these things will be given to you as well.

Matthew 6:33

The LORD detests dishonest scales, but accurate weights find favor with him.

Proverbs 11:1

No one can serve two masters. Either you will hate the one and love the other, or you will be devoted to the one and despise the other. You cannot serve both God and money.

Matthew 6:24

In all your ways submit to him, and he will make your paths straight.

Proverbs 3:6

And God spoke all these words: 'I am the LORD your God, who brought you out of Egypt, out of the land of slavery. You shall have no other gods before me.'

Exodus 20:1–3

For the grace of God has appeared that offers salvation to all people. It teaches us to say "No" to ungodliness and worldly passions, and to live self-controlled, upright and godly lives in this present age.

Titus 2:11–12

Therefore, dear friends, since you have been forewarned, be on your guard so that you may not be carried away by the error of the lawless and fall from your secure position.

2 Peter 3:17

By the seventh day God had finished the work he had been doing; so on the seventh day he rested from all his work. Then God blessed the seventh day and made it holy, because on it he rested from all the work of creating that he had done.

Genesis 2:2–3

And without faith it is impossible to please God, because anyone who comes to him must believe that he exists and the he rewards those who earnestly seek him.

Hebrews 11:6

'Love the Lord your God with all your heart and with all your soul and with all your strength and with all your mind'; and, 'Love your neighbor as yourself.'

Luke 10:27

STRESS

Most of the struggles we deal with lead to this particular struggle, which is stress, and it is a big one. We all deal with some sort of stress on most days of our lives. Stress comes at us in many forms, such as anxiety, tension, burdens, worry, agony, fear, finances, hardships, hassles, nervousness, trauma, business, and so many more things we have to deal with. It tends to strike us in times where we are the most vulnerable such as when we have too much going on at once in our lives or in times when we are struggling or hurting emotionally. It can overcome you and can quickly spin out of control. When you reach the point where stress builds up quickly at one time, or on top of other things, it can cause serious mental and physical health problems.

Stress is proven to raise blood pressure and heart rates, cause heavier breathing, cause tension in your body and muscles, decrease your immune system, slow down your digestive system, prevent sleep, just to name some of the effects it can have on you physically. Mentally, it can lessen your sense of awareness and alertness, cause anger, cause anxiety, leave you feeling sad or depressed, cause forgetfulness and fatigue, and make you irritable and burnt out. It is one of the most detrimental struggles that we put ourselves through.

The bad part of stress is that it has no fingerprint, meaning it can affect everyone differently. What causes stress on you may not even affect someone else. How one person deals with their stress can also be completely different from someone else. Stress can come from something actually happening, or it can just be the thought of something that stresses you out. It is such a powerful weapon for Satan.

Let me give you some alarming statistics about stress in the current state of this Hellven world we live in from the American Institute of Stress. One in five people experiences extreme stress with symptoms such as shaking, heart palpitations, or depression. Three out of four doctor's visits are for stress-related ailments. Stress is the basic cause of 60 percent of all human illnesses and diseases. Stress increases heart disease by 40 percent, increases the risk of heart attack by 25 percent, and increases the risk of stroke by 50 percent. At least 40 percent of stressed people overeat or eat unhealthy foods. At least 44 percent of stressed people lose sleep every night. Stress is just getting worse and worse, too, because 44 percent of people feel more stressed now than they did just five years ago. These are just some examples. Can you just picture Satan laughing and rubbing his hands together over this? Here we all are, living as part of these statistics, though.

Stress is something that I definitely deal with all of the time. I am a construction project manager, which makes the list of the topmost stressful jobs. On top of that, I am an executive in my company, which is also on the list. In addition to my job stress, I have some other major things going on in my personal and family life, which you will hear in other chapters that really add to my stress level. Some people that know me well often tell me that they don't know how I handle everything. They want to know how I do it. Well, I will tell you that I sometimes wonder the same things. I am also that person that holds everything in and bottles it all up, so I have trouble releasing my stress and expressing my feelings. I've always been that way, and I can't really help it, but it sure makes things even harder on me by not dealing with things properly.

So how do we deal with stress in our lives? Well, because God created us, He knows us perfectly and knows that we, too, often allow Satan to release stressors all around and on us. So, God has given us some great ways to deal with stress. I have said it in other chapters already, but we first have to trust in God and understand that He wants to help us through every situation and rid our lives of stressors. God gave us the most powerful tool to deal with stress and every other struggle for that matter, which is His Son, Jesus Christ. Jesus is always there for us and gives us help and encouragement in all we are going through. Sometimes when we feel like there is no one or nothing on earth that can help us through our stress and troubles, only Jesus can provide that peace and strength that we need to get through it all. All it takes is trusting in Him and believing that He will be the relief that we need. It's a lot easier said than done, and unless you experience it for yourself, I understand it can sound a bit hard to believe, but you have to take that first step and just surrender all of your stress and worries to Jesus. Believing and trusting in Him is not a magical act that will suddenly make everything stressing you out disappear, but you will notice that those things will begin to fade out because you are putting your efforts and thoughts into better things. Jesus is always there for us, waiting and ready to listen and hear our worries and troubles. Even us that hold things in and don't share our stressors with others can at least lean on the Lord and cast our burdens upon Him. So, believe in Him, confide in Him, and trust in Him for deliverance from your stress, and you will find true peace in your life. By doing these things, God's love, grace, and mercy will be released upon you, and your stress will be less and less until it is gone.

As Christians, trusting in God for stress relief is the first and most important thing to do, but there are also things we can do ourselves to help our situation and provide relief as well. God gives us intelligence so that we can make smart decisions when faced with stressful situations. Take control of things and be smart by trying to remove yourself from situations or distance yourself from things or people that trigger your stress. Manage your time and plan out your day so that you can prioritize the things you have going on. Sometimes you have to realize that some things are more important than others, and you have to let go of some things. Try not to overload yourself when you feel overwhelmed. When you have too much going on at one time, it's okay to say "no." Embrace the fact that you can't always please everyone at all times and that it's okay too. That doesn't mean that you have to ignore responsibilities; it just means that it may take you a little longer sometimes to get to all of them.

Another thing you can do is simply talk about things and not bottle them up. Like I said earlier, I tend to bottle my stress, and it only makes it harder to deal with. I have learned that talking about things is much better. Simply talking about the stress in your life can help release some of it that you have bottled up. It can also help by distracting you from the thoughts that are constantly on your mind. Find someone that is a good listener and lean on them, whether it's a spouse, a good friend, a co-worker, or even a counselor if you are more comfortable with a neutral person. I'm a very quiet guy a lot of the time because I am just not comfortable talking about some things or to some people, but I have talked to counselors, and it has helped me. I also confide in my wife, who is my best friend and my safe place. She helps me tremendously and always seems to have the perfect things to say to calm me down and give me some needed relief from my thoughts and stress.

Then there are physical things you can do. First, try to avoid the consumption of things that have been proven to increase stress levels, such as caffeine, nicotine, and alcohol. Try to drink decaffeinated coffee or caffeine sodas. Drink more water and stay hydrated with healthier things. Next, you can try to be more active. If you don't already make time in your busy schedule to do some sort of workout, then either try to make time for it or at least try to figure out ways to get more active in your daily routine. Take the stairs instead of the elevator. Take a break and walk around your office. Any new activities you can think of will help. Getting more physical during your day will, in turn, help you get better sleep at night too, which is another thing that you need to try to do. Work on your nightly routine and try to improve your sleep habits. Try to get in bed earlier if you can and spend a little time reading or something that gives your thoughts a chance to slow down. Take a warm bath or shower to relax your body. Anything you can do to help relax your body and mind to help get you to a place of comfort and peace of mind will greatly improve your sleep, which will decrease stress levels in your life tremendously.

> *Do not be anxious about anything, but in every situation, by prayer and petition, with thanksgiving, present your requests to God.*
>
> **Philippians 4:6**

Peace I leave with you; my peace I give you. I do not give to you as the world gives. Do not let your hearts be troubled and do not be afraid.

John 14:27

When hard pressed, I cried to the Lord; he brought me into a spacious place. The Lord is with me; I will not be afraid. What can mere mortals do to me?

Psalm 118:5–6

Come to me, all you who are weary and burdened, and I will give you rest. Take my yoke upon you and learn from me, for I am gentle and humble in heart, and you will find rest for your souls. For my yoke is easy and my burden is light.

Matthew 11:28–30

God is our refuge and strength, an ever-present help in trouble.

Psalm 46:1

He gives strength to the weary and increases the power of the weak. Even youths grow tired and weary, and young men stumble and fail; but those who hope in the LORD will renew their strength. They will soar on wings like eagles; they will run and not grow weary, they will walk and not be faint.

Isaiah 40:29–31

I have told you these things, so that in me you may have peace. In this world you will have trouble. But take heart! I have overcome the world.

John 16:33

And my God will meet all your needs according to the riches of his glory in Christ Jesus.

Philippians 4:19

As for everyone who comes to me and hears my words and puts them into practice, I will show you what they are like. They are like a man building a house, who dug down deep and laid the foundation on rock. When a flood came, the torrent struck that house but could not shake it, because it was well built.

Luke 6:47–48

So do not fear, for I am with you; do not be dismayed, for I am your God. I will strengthen you and help you; I will uphold you with my righteous right hand.

Isaiah 41:10

DEPRESSION

When we live in a world where sin rules and Satan has his way with us, one of the main results is depression. The word "depression" has a few meanings, and each of them shows the characteristics that Satan inflicts on the world. The definition that we want to look at is the "emotional depression," but I also want you to see the other definitions too so you can really understand the word itself.

One definition is "the angular distance of a celestial object below the horizon." The word used in this context explains low places in the terrain of the land, such as valleys, canyons, or lowlands. All of these are the lowest places you can physically get on this earth. Another common definition for depression is "a period of low general economic activity marked especially by rising levels of unemployment and struggle." Our country has gone through periods like this, such as the "Great Depression," which happened from 1929 to 1939 and was the deepest and longest-lasting economic period in history. I'm sure you have learned about this period in school and remember stories of how hard it was to live through. Then you have the most commonly used definition of depression, which is "a state of feeling of deep sadness marked by inactivity, difficulty in thinking and concentration, a significant increase or decrease in appetite and time spent sleeping, feelings of dejection and hopelessness, and sometimes suicidal tendencies." Now look at those three definitions and just think about how powerful they can be as a tool for Satan to use, especially in Hellven. Depression is the very air we breathe in Hellven, and that is why it runs rampant, creeping and climbing everywhere it can with the goal of covering everything and everyone completely.

Millions of people, Christians and non-Christians, struggle with depression throughout their lives. Some people struggle with it daily. Satan will take advantage of anything that happens in your life that could trigger depression for you, such as the loss of a job, the loss of a loved one, a divorce or breakup of a relationship, financial problems, or even psychological problems such as low self-esteem or any form of abuse.

Once Satan gets his foot in the door with these triggers and depression sets in, he then turns his attention to your thoughts and feelings. He uses the depression to make you resent others, turn from God, and break you down physically. Before you know it, you will find yourself feeling guilty all the time, doubting everything, worrying constantly, always complaining, and feeling hopeless. You will either overeat and gain lots of weight, or not eat at all and become very unhealthy and weak. You will distance yourself from others and reject those around you who clearly see the signs of depression and just want to help you. You will end up digging yourself into a hole that you feel you will not be able to get out of, and that is exactly where Satan wants you to be.

If you have been through depression in your life or are going through it now, then these things will be all too familiar to you. If you haven't struggled with depression yourself, but you have seen others around you go through it and not understand it, then I think it is important to understand that everyone is different. Some of us can have something happen in our lives, and we can bounce right back from it and be fine, but others of us may go through the same thing and fall into depression. We all think differently, feel differently, and can be attacked differently. It is easy to write someone off as weak that is struggling with depression and think that it couldn't happen to you, but we are all capable of falling into it.

Depression can hit anyone at any time. I am all too familiar with it myself as it has dwelled in my house like a fog for the past several years. My own son, Donovan, struggled with depression, as well as a bipolar disorder on top of it, which only intensified his depression when he would hit lows. His depression put him into a deep, dark, and heavy place. It seemed to take over his soul and affected everything about him. It affected his health, his attitude, and his decisions. It put him in a place where he felt all of his goals and dreams were out of reach. He pushed loved ones away and wouldn't let anyone help him, and he wouldn't help himself either. When we could talk him into getting some help, nothing really seemed to pull him out of it and keep him there. It was like a living, breathing monster that sucked the life out of him.

I want to point out that around the age of sixteen, my son surrendered to the ministry and wanted to be a youth pastor. He had been really involved with his youth program at our church and was trying to be there every time the doors were open or be a part of everything he could to serve. He had a passion for helping others and loved to speak to others about the Lord. Soon after, he made that decision is when his depression and problems started. I fully believe that is when Satan crept in and started a spiritual war in Donovan's life.

The truth is, when someone here on earth makes a decision to lead others to Christ, Satan erupts with anger and fear against that person and concentrates on stopping it. Here in Hellven, it doesn't take much effort for Satan to win that battle. Satan has command of this earthly realm and has been building up his power over us more and more as we have become a culture that has allowed him to. Unfortunately, it makes it even harder for us to battle things like depression and all of the many other struggles we all face.

On March 21, 2016, Donovan ended up taking his own life. It was the worst day imaginable and pushed me, my wife, and my two daughters into our own depression. Even as years have now passed since we lost him, we are still battling with our own depression over the loss. My oldest daughter turned to drugs to try to deal with things, got into some trouble, and ended up in juvenile detention and other issues from not properly dealing with things. My younger daughter later spent time as an inpatient at a mental health hospital as she had been struggling with suicidal thoughts and her own depression from losing her brother and not having her sister around. My wife and I found ourselves sitting in a quiet house that once was filled with the noises of three happy kids, and we were simply trying to hold it together and survive. Depression felt like quicksand in our house that we were unable to escape.

In the midst of all of this, though, I want to share that we still hold fast to the promises of God and know that He is going to restore our family and us. My wife and I held each other's hands and prayed together and agreed that we would believe in God for resurrection for our family, and we agreed that we would not let Satan win the battle over our family. I want you to know that soon after that, our youngest daughter told us that she had prayed for the first time in a very long time and asked Jesus to forgive her for being mad at Him and for not talking to Him for a long time. She told us that she sees the underlying issues and is dealing with them and that she wants to get back on the right track. Around that time, we also had a family counseling session at the juvenile detention center with our older daughter, where she started talking about studying her Bible and that she is also now seeking the Lord again for her help and strength. I truly believe that our faith is all that has kept my wife and me able to keep our heads above water through all of this. Sometimes when I talk about it like I am right now, I am even amazed that we have been able to survive it all.

The facts are that about 25 percent of the population are either going through depression right now or have been depressed at some point. The world's current population is about seven billion, so 25 percent of that is 1.75 billion people. That is a whole lot of depression, and Satan and his army are having a field day with it.

So, with that much depression, what can we do to help ourselves or those around us get out of it? First and most importantly, we have to recognize that God does not want us to live a depressing life; He wants us to live a joyful life. I truly believe that things like depression are spiritual attacks and that part of overcoming them is simply turning to God for help. That means getting on your knees in prayer, getting into His Word and studying scriptures, getting in church and surrounding yourself with other Christians, and leaning fully on God to lift you up out of the depression. Just simply showing Satan that you are a child of God and that you do not accept being drug down by him is half the battle. If the depression is not too deep, these first steps can be enough to pull you out and get you back on track.

If the depression is deeper and darker, there are other steps that can be taken, such as seeing a good Christian counselor, a physician, or even a psychiatrist. I think it is important to make sure they are Christian, though. Otherwise, you open yourself up to being fed more Hellven lies, which will continue to keep you down. God gives each and every one of us gifts and skills that He intends for us to use to help each other. If you take steps to get help from Christian counselors or doctors, then you are putting yourself in a position for God to work through them to help you overcome the deeper depression you may be in. It is also important to understand that depression can sometimes be linked to a physical or mental disorder, which definitely requires being diagnosed and treated by a doctor, and it is okay. In those cases, treating the depression or disorder is no different than going to a doctor because you are sick with a cold or the flu. My entire family has been seeing counselors, psychiatrists and taking classes here and there for this entire past year and a half, and we will continue to do what we can to help us push through it. You have to use the resources that are available to you.

If you are not dealing with depression yourself but have a friend or loved one that is, I urge you to take it seriously. Understand that it is a real struggle for them and lift them up in prayer daily. Pray specifically for God to remove the stronghold that Satan has on them through the depression. Pray for their spiritual eyes to be opened so that they may see God as the light to guide them out of the darkness. Ask God to bring His true joy and peace back into their life. Reach out to them and show them love and support in any and every way you can. Urge them to seek help and medication if needed. Encourage them to get into Scripture and church and to fellowship with other Christians. When they feel like giving up on life, let them know you are not giving up on them. Just being there for them on a consistent basis, even if they push you away, will let them see you really care. Be an ear to hear their pain, a shoulder to cry on when they need it, and assure them of God's love for them.

Depression does not have to be a permanent condition. In God, there is healing and hope. God's grace and love are more powerful than anything or any struggle, and even in this dark world where the darkness of depression is so camouflaged, God is our light. Rejoice in Him and let His light shine through you.

National Suicide Prevention Lifeline—24/7

Call 1–800–273–8255 if you or anyone you know is struggling with suicidal thoughts.

Answer me quickly, LORD; my spirit fails. Do not hide your face from me or I will be like those who go down to the pit. Let the morning bring me word of your unfailing love, for I have put my trust in you. Show me the way I should go, for to you I entrust my life.

Psalm 143:7–8

May the God of hope fill you with all joy and peace as you trust in him, so that you may overflow with hope by the power of the Holy Spirit.

Romans 15:13

The LORD is a refuge for the oppressed, a stronghold in times of trouble.

Psalm 9:9

Even youths grow tired and weary, and young men stumble and fall; but those who hope in the LORD will renew their strength. They will soar on wings like eagles; they will run and not grow weary, they will walk and not be faint.

Isaiah 40:30–31

I waited patiently for the LORD; he turned to me and heard my cry. He lifted me out of the slimy pit, out of the mud and mire; he set my feet on a rock and gave me a firm place to stand.

Psalm 40:1–2

Arise, shine, for your light has come, and the glory of the LORD rises upon you. See, darkness covers the earth and thick darkness is over the peoples, but the LORD rises upon you and his glory appears over you.

Isaiah 60:1–2

You, LORD, are my lamp; the LORD turns my darkness into light.

2 Samuel 22:29

I am laid low in the dust; preserve my life according to your word.

Psalm 119:25

The LORD himself goes before you and will be with you; he will never leave you nor forsake you. Do not be afraid; do not be discouraged.

Deuteronomy 31:8

I have told you these things, so that in me you may have peace. In this world you will have trouble. But take heart! I have overcome the world.

John 16:33

GRIEF

Grief is a struggle that hurts like no other. The definition of "grief" is "keen mental suffering or distress over loss; sharp sorrow; painful regret; keen distress or sorrow." I am not sure that words can even describe it, though. It is not only an emotional thing, but it is physically draining as well. Going through true grief can be one of the hardest things you will ever do in your life on earth.

As I mentioned in the last chapter, my family is in the midst of what I feel has to be the hardest grief there is, which is the loss of a child. Not to take away from anyone's own loss, whether it was the loss of a spouse, a mother, a father, a grandparent, a sibling, or a close friend, but I think losing a child has to hurt the most. Then I think losing a child to suicide raises the grief bar other several notches. My wife and I have had many conversations about how it would have been easier to lose him in an accident or any other way because this way just stings worse. It has caused many struggles on top of normal grief, such as guilt and thoughts of failure, which lead to a deeper depression than typical grief can cause. You have probably heard about "stages of grief" and heard all kinds of teaching and preaching on grief, but I say that once you have experienced true grief, you may laugh at everything you have heard or learned about it prior because it is just a beast that can't be categorized or stepped through very easily. It is a constant, daily struggle that doesn't go away, no matter which stage you find yourself in. My family has to live with it now, and we all deal with it in our own ways, but it still hurts each of us the same. We have some days that are easier than others, but some days you will feel numb to the world, and you don't even want to move or get out of bed. Some days you find yourself so emotionally sad and full of sorrow that you can't stop crying. Some days you find yourself ticked off at the world over the loss, and you just want to punch happy people in the face. Petty things of this world become so annoying, and noise becomes magnified in your ears like never before. Things that never bothered you will now be some of your pet peeves. Things you liked before, you may hate now. Holidays, birthdays, and special times become days you dread or avoid. The best way to explain the feeling is that you just don't fit into the world around you any longer. It's just draining, emotionally and physically.

I spend countless hours just thinking about times where I could have said or done something differently and possibly changed something. I beat myself up over the little things. I have flashbacks of every single time I feel I failed my son as a father. I battle with the "what ifs" daily. I stare at pictures of him and remember each moment that was captured. I watch old videos just to hear his voice and his laugh. I see visions of him walking down the stairs of our house or him walking down the sidewalk in our neighborhood like I so often saw. These things are just constantly on my mind and in my thoughts.

I also recently lost my father to COVID-19, which has just compounded my grief personally. As far as guys go in my immediate family, I only had my dad, my brother, and my son. I've now lost two of them unexpectantly, and it hurts like no other pain I could ever describe. I often find myself wanting to talk to one of them so badly about something, but I realize I can't. I don't know how many times I have picked up the phone to call my dad and then realize he's not there to answer, or I want to call out for my son to come downstairs to watch a movie or something with me, and he's not there. I often find myself trying not to believe it is real that they are really gone, but they are, and it just plain sucks.

I wish I had the perfect answer for dealing with grief, but I don't think there can be just one perfect answer for it. If there was, none of us would be going through it with such pain. As a believer, though, there is one perfect word for dealing with it, and that is *hope*. Even in my pain and sorrow, I can tell you that I have the hope that God gives us. I can tell you that my son was saved, and I hold fast to what God says about that. In John 10:28–30,

Jesus says: "I give them eternal life, and they shall never perish; no one will snatch them out of my hand. My Father, who has given them to me, is greater than all; no one can snatch them out of my Father's hand. I and the Father are one." I feel like things of this world and Satan crept in and tried to take my son over, but ultimately, they failed because no power could snatch my son away from God, and he is there with our Lord now. No matter what I feel or am going through, I do know that I will be there with God too one day and will be reunited with my son, as well as all of my other loved ones that were and are believers.

I also want to share some things with you that have been helping my family as well and give you some things you can do, watch for, and pray for to help you through your grief. First, I want you to know and understand that it's okay to grieve. It's okay to be upset, to be mad, to cry, or to feel any way you need or want to feel. One of the best pieces of advice my wife and I got was when a good friend told us to "be selfish in our grief." That may sound odd, but it has sure helped our outlook and given us some relief. Everyone is going to grieve differently, so you have to deal with things in your own way and not worry about what others think or do and not worry about how you look to anyone else. Being selfish in your grief just means that you will not let others tell you how to act or how to feel, and you will not allow anyone to push you through the process. You shouldn't do anything during your grief that you don't want to do. Sometimes that will mean that you might hurt the feelings of friends or family by making them feel distant, but as long as you don't do it sinfully, there is nothing wrong with it. If someone hasn't felt true loss or grief, then they just won't understand what you are going through, and there is nothing you can do to make them understand. People will come from every direction to give you advice or tell you to do this or that, and you will just have to do what you think is best for you. There will also be things that may be good for you, but not your spouse or other family members. You have to remember to let everyone handle their grief as they need to. This is just one thing in your life that I believe you should be selfish in because no one on this earth can know exactly how you feel and what you are going through. Only God can do that.

The next thing I want to share is that as Christians, we have something that non-believers have in our grief. We have a loving, caring heavenly Father that wants to comfort us and give us peace. We need to understand that God knows the sorrow that we go through and that He hurts to see us go through grief. Remember that God Himself knows loss. We all know John 3:16: "For God so loved the world that he gave his one and only Son, that whoever believes in him shall not perish but have eternal life." He knows the loss of a child because He gave His Son up for all of us. He sees and feels every loss any of us ever go through, and He wants to help us through those times. Even when Jesus was here on the earth, He experienced grief. John, chapter 11, talks about Jesus seeing Mary and others that are grieving the death of Lazarus, that He Himself was troubled, that He groaned in the spirit, and that He even wept with them. That does not mean that Jesus did not have faith; He simply was full of love and wept with those who weep in love.

In our grief, my wife and I were introduced to something some friends of ours who have also lost a son calls "God's kisses," which is just another name for how God shows His love for us in our grief. "God's kisses" are some of the most precious things we have experienced in our grief, and they are simply moments that God reveals things to you that cause you to know without a doubt that it came from Him. We have received "God's kisses" often since our son died, and many are very personal, but I just want to share a few to show the power and love of God. The thing with them is that God gives them specifically to each individual, so they will mean the most to that person, but they are still neat to hear from others.

My wife and I both have gotten to hear our son's voice multiple times. Mostly during prayer or while in church, but also at various other times. The first time for me was while we were standing in church during worship time one week, fairly close to the time after he died. The song we were singing was a slow song and had me emotional. I prayed to God and just asked Him to hug my son and tell him how much I love him and miss him. I immediately heard my son's voice as if he was whispering it in my ear say, "I love you and Mom both so much, Dad." Another time I woke up about an hour before my alarm was to go off. I couldn't really go back to sleep, so I just lay there. All of a sudden, the song "Blessed Assurance" started playing in my head. I hadn't even really heard that song in years, as churches these days don't play the old hymns as much. I felt strongly impressed to listen to the words of that song, so on my way to work that morning, I looked it up on Youtube and listened to it on repeat on my drive to work. As I was listening to it, I could literally hear my son saying to me, "This is exactly the words that I want you and mom to hear right now: 'Blessed assurance, Jesus is mine! I'm purchased of God and washed in His blood. This is my story; this is my song. I'm praising my Savior all day long. I, in my Savior, am happy and blest. Watching and waiting, looking above, filled with His goodness, lost in His love.'" Needless to say, I was overcome with peace and emotion and had to compose myself before going into the office that morning, but it was such a powerful thing for God to bless me with. Even in just sharing moments like this between my wife and me, we have been blessed so much, and we are so thankful for them.

"God's kisses" have also come in the form of getting to see our son. God has revealed our son to Amanda on multiple occasions where he is running in beautiful fields, singing, and telling her how much he loves her. I have been given similar visions of him walking down what looked like beautiful corridors of a massive building while talking to me. The neat thing is, when we both described our separate visions to each other, we found that our son looked like he was about fifteen or sixteen years old to both of us. He was twenty-two when he died. We had exact common characteristics and details that were not coincident. God uses moments like these to comfort us by showing us that our son is happier than he has ever been and that he is there with Him waiting for us.

There are also "God's kisses" in small things daily if we open our eyes and ears to them, even as subtle as they can be. One morning driving to work, I was beating myself up over whether or not I was a good enough father to my son. I turned on the radio, and the very first words I heard were, "You're a good, good father" from a Christian song that was playing. That song is referring to our heavenly Father, but God gave me that small thing that delivered me from a moment of pain that morning. Speaking of songs, God has used songs over and over to help us as well. Some song that we heard a hundred times before will come on the radio, and it will speak to us like we never heard it before and will seem like it was written just for us. We have many songs that we cherish now because of it. We will also just be driving down the street or walking in the mall or something, and we will see things that will remind us of our son and make us smile or laugh, and we get joy out of it. There are just so many "God's kisses" that we have been given. We even started a journal to write them all down in so we won't forget them and can go back to them when we are having a bad day. Journaling is something I recommend to anyone who is going through grief of any kind. It helps to put your thoughts down or to keep memories or "God's kisses" so you can always have them.

Another thing I want to suggest in dealing with your grief is to find godly people that have been through the same grief you are going through. It helps to be exactly the same grief as every type of loss can be different. Since our loss was a suicide, there were all kinds of groups and people reaching out to help us when it happened. One of the biggest blessings we had was a few days after when a couple of people from a suicide outreach group for our county stopped by our house. There was a man that came who had also lost a son to suicide, and he just wanted us to know we were not alone. These people take time out of their busy schedules and from dealing with their own grief just to help others in their shoes, and it amazed us. The man ended up coming back to our house a couple of times and constantly would reach out to me by text or email, and we have become good friends. He is always there for me if I just need to talk to and we actually ended up leaning on each other quite a bit and still do. We then set up a small group of couples that had lost children and began getting together once a month for dinner and sharing stories and "God's kisses." We all laugh some, and we cry some. There is nothing that has helped us more than to be with those couples as they know the exact things we are feeling and going through, and it just blesses us so much. When someone close to you dies, you will have hundreds of people giving condolences and telling you things and trying to act like they could guess what you are feeling, but the truth is, unless they have had that exact type of loss, they just can't understand. It's hard to even listen to most people talk to you that haven't been through it, even though you know they are just trying to help. Unfortunately, it will mostly just get on your nerves, and sometimes you will want to just tell them to shut up. When you are talking to those who can relate, though, it is just different as you can share exact, common feelings and thoughts, so I suggest reaching out and trying to meet others in the same boat if you can. I think God even sends us to each other as He knows we all need it. It's also neat to see that someone God sends to help you can also end up getting helped themselves by you in return. I thank God for our small group of grieving parents.

The bottom line is that grief is one of life's most challenging and painful struggles. It can literally rip your heart out and tear up relationships if you let it. I wouldn't wish this pain on anyone and couldn't imagine anything being worse on this earth than going through the grief we are currently in with my family. It just plain sucks. We all just have to hold fast to our faith and hope in the Lord and look forward to the day we are reunited with our loved ones, as we are promised in God's Word. Every day we spend here on earth is a day we are closer to that reunion. We just have to keep on living and realize that we are still here for a purpose and that God is not finished with us yet. Let God use your experience to help others, and you will find some peace in it.

> *The righteous cry out, and the LORD hears them; he delivers them from all their troubles. The LORD is close to the brokenhearted and saves those who are crushed in spirit. The righteous person may have many troubles, but the LORD delivers him from them all.*
>
> **Psalm 34:17–19**

> *He will wipe every tear from their eyes. There will be no more death or mourning or crying or pain, for the old order of things has passed away.*
>
> **Revelation 21:4**

> *Praise be to the God and Father of our Lord Jesus Christ, the Father of compassion and the God of all comfort, who comforts us in all our troubles, so that we can comfort those in any trouble with the comfort we ourselves receive from God.*
>
> **2 Corinthians 1:3–4**

> *He heals the brokenhearted and binds up their wounds.*
>
> **Psalm 147:3**

> *In a little while you will see me no more, and then after a little while you will see me.*
>
> **John 16:16**

Weeping may stay for the night, but rejoicing comes in the morning.

Psalm 30:5

Brothers and sisters, we do not want you to be uninformed about those who sleep in death, so that you do not grieve like the rest of mankind, who have no hope. For we believe that Jesus died and rose again, and so we believe that God will bring with Jesus those who have fallen asleep in him.

1 Thessalonians 4:13–14

Blessed are those who mourn, for they will be comforted.

Matthew 5:4

Rejoice with those who rejoice; mourn with those who mourn.

Romans 12:15

The righteous perish, and no one takes it to heart; the devout are taken away, and no one understands that the righteous are taken away to be spared from evil. Those who walk uprightly enter into peace; they find rest as they lie in death.

Isaiah 57:1–2

ADDICTION

Addiction is a struggle that can come in many forms and hit anyone. It is such a complex and massive tool that Satan uses these days. Some of the main addictions that we see are drugs and alcohol, sex or pornography, gambling or spending money, and food or unhealthy eating habits, just to name a few. Addictions can be physical, mental, or both. It is actually defined as a "brain disorder that is characterized by compulsive engagement in rewarding stimuli, despite adverse consequences." So basically, it means we get addicted to things that are detrimental to our health; we know it's bad for us or our relationships, yet we keep on doing it over and over until we either find a way to break it or it breaks us. Am I the only one that can see Satan's hand all over this? It also sounds just like today's Christians as we are all doing things we know we should not be doing, yet we just keep on keeping on. Maybe it's that we are addicted to sin here in Hellven. That is a deeper thought, but I will get back to addiction.

Just like many of the struggles we have already talked about, addiction is an epidemic across the world. In my studies on addiction statistics, I have found many alarming things that prove how powerful addiction is. Here are a few of them to think about. About 240 million people worldwide are dependent on alcohol. More than a billion people smoke. About fifteen million people use injection drugs, such as heroin. Here in the United States, over 200 million people over the age of twelve have an addiction. One hundred people die every day from a drug overdose, and this rate has tripled in the past twenty years. Almost seven million people with an addiction also have a mental illness. People between the ages of eighteen and twenty-five have the highest addiction rates, even though addiction has no limits on age. Approximately 187,000 people worldwide die each year from drug overdose. Almost 3.5 million deaths each year worldwide are attributed to alcohol, whether directly or indirectly. Over 300,000 deaths each year in the US are attributed to obesity and food addiction. More than one million sexually transmitted infections are acquired every day worldwide.

If the addiction doesn't kill the person directly, it can all lead to other complications and struggles, such as depression or major health problems. These things can also put a person on a path to death. We have already mentioned how depression is the number one cause of suicide deaths in a previous chapter, but did you know that addicts of any kind are six times more likely to take their own lives than anyone else? Just researching and writing all of this is depressing. It is easy to see what a huge struggle addiction is in our world. You can't even watch five minutes of your local news without hearing some sort of story that is linked to an addict.

It's also important to point out that no one is immune to addiction. It can hit anyone at any age. For starters, almost half a million babies are born each year with an addiction to at least one substance because of their mother's addictions. These babies are born into addiction without choice. Addiction can also hit people that you would least expect, such as pastors or other care professionals that would seem to be immune to it. I think looking at pastor statistics gets the point across the best, though. Based on studies by Pastoral Care Inc., four in ten pastors view pornography daily. Food addiction and obesity is the number one health problem with pastors. Ninety percent of pastors are workaholics and work between fifty-five to seventy-five hours per week. One in every ten people are dealing with addiction of some form, so just look at the people you interact with every day and think about that statistic. You will see all kinds of people, all ages of people, and all ethnicities of people are affected by this epidemic struggle. You may also find yourself as the addict or part of this epidemic, but as you can see, you are not alone.

I have told you already that I was raised a preacher's kid and was actually a pretty good kid, not getting into much trouble growing up. My wife and I both were raised in church, and neither of us really messed with drugs or alcohol. Even with our backgrounds and the fact that we feel like we raised our kids to have the same values and beliefs that we have, two out of three of our kids have battled drug addiction, and our third kid has been affected by it in an extreme way. We have all been affected by it. It ultimately helped lead to the death of our son. My wife and I have often wondered how or why this happened to our kids since we didn't bring them up around drugs or addiction, yet here we are caught in its web with our family. Again, we are all vulnerable to addiction, no matter who we are or how we have been brought up.

Some addiction is caused by mental illness or sickness and sometimes can't be avoided when the person can't think for themselves clearly, but I would venture to say that in most cases of addiction, it is not a sickness, but rather a sin problem that gets us hooked. Identifying that you ultimately have a sin problem is a critical first step to conquering your addictions. There is good news in that because Jesus conquers sin, and He can deliver you from your addictions. Just like the other struggles we have already talked about, seeking help from Jesus has got to be a priority. Sometimes when you can't admit your addictions to the people in your life, it is easier to first pray and confess your sins to Jesus and let Him give you peace and comfort, which will lead to having the courage to open up to others and get help. Once you can seek help, God will open the right doors and help guide you to the right people or places where you can get treatment and help you overcome the physical and mental demands of your addiction.

I will tell you, though, that unless you truly surrender your addiction to God and repent, and then make the absolute choice that you will no longer be a slave to whatever addiction you have, you will never be able to overcome it. You have to make the true choice that you will change your heart and mind away from the things that have you trapped. That sometimes means a whole new life path. Sometimes it means abandoning family or friends that are not a healthy influence on you. Sometimes it means a new job or a new town to live in where you can get away from temptations. You have to separate yourself from your addiction, separate yourself from your sin. If the people around you do not build you up, then you don't need to associate yourself with them. These can be some easy, life-changing ways to get yourself on the right path to recovery that you can do yourself.

There are also a ton of ways to get professional help if your addictions are too heavy for you to handle on your own. Nowadays, since addiction is such an epidemic, there are treatment facilities for all types of addiction. There are outpatient and inpatient facilities. There are classes you can take in person or online. There are programs of all types that you can get involved with. There are also mentoring and partnering programs where you can get an accountability partner to be there for you when you don't have someone. A majority of our churches now have recovery programs and groups that meet to help with addictions. It will absolutely help you to get into a facility or a group and see that you are not alone. You can hear other people that are going through the same things you are and feel more comfortable talking about your problems with them because you feel that they understand you and what you are going through. People that are trained or have experienced addiction themselves will be able to offer you the best advice and tell you what helped them the most.

So, addictions are a very powerful struggle, but they are not impossible to overcome. Seek God and lean on Him first and then allow Him to direct you to a path that will lead you to freedom from your addiction. He will put you where you need to be and around the right people to help you. He will give you strength and offer you peace and protection. In Him, you will find your freedom.

> *No temptation has overtaken you except what is common to mankind. And God is faithful; he will not let you be tempted beyond what you can bear. But when you are tempted, he will also provide a way out so that you can endure it.*
>
> **1 Corinthians 10:13**

> *Be alert and of sober mind. Your enemy the devil prowls around like a roaring lion looking for someone to devour. Resist him,*

standing firm in the faith, because you know that the family of believers throughout the world is undergoing the same kind of sufferings. And the God of all grace, who called you to his eternal glory in Christ, after you have suffered a little while, will himself restore you and make you strong, firm and steadfast.

1 Peter 5:8–10

Submit yourselves, then, to God. Resist the devil, and he will flee from you.

James 4:7

Not only so, but we also glory in our sufferings, because we know that suffering produces perseverance; perseverance, character; and character, hope. And hope does not put us to shame, because God's love has been poured out into our hearts through the Holy Spirit, who has been given to us.

Romans 5:3–5

For we do not have a high priest who is unable to empathize with our weaknesses, but we have one who has been tempted in every way, just as we are—yet he did not sin. Let us then approach God's throne of grace with confidence, so that we may receive mercy and find grace to help us in our time of need.

Hebrews 4:15–16

I can do all this through him who gives me strength.

Philippians 4:13

Watch and pray so that you will not fall into temptation. The spirit is willing, but the flesh is weak.

Matthew 26:41

Wine is a mocker and beer a brawler; whoever is led astray by them is not wise.

Proverbs 20:1

It is for freedom that Christ has set us free. Stand firm, then, and do not let yourselves be burdened again by a yoke of slavery.

Galatians 5:1

Blessed is the one who perseveres under trial because, having stood the test, that person will receive the crown of life that the Lord has promised to those who love him. When tempted, no one should say, 'God is tempting me.' For God cannot be tempted by evil, nor does he tempt anyone; but each person is tempted when they are dragged away by their own evil desire and enticed. Then, after desire has conceived, it gives birth to sin; and sin, when it is full-grown, gives birth to death.

James 1:12–15

HONESTY AND INTEGRITY

Being honest and having integrity are two important keys to really growing spiritually and growing into the person you are meant to be. Honesty is a quality that gives you a real sense of sincerity to those around you. Integrity goes with honesty as it is a quality of being honest and gives you a sense of having strong moral principles to those around you. Integrity is doing the right thing every time, no matter what the circumstances or consequences are. Having these qualities allows others to put trust in you and makes them feel comfortable around you.

Unfortunately, these days we can find it harder and harder to find people with these qualities, and we can find ourselves personally lacking these qualities as well. We live in a deceitful world. Satan is the master at deceit and wants to spread his lies, and we stand here ready to hear his lies and help him spread them. People have gotten so far from these qualities that sometimes it feels like you can't trust anyone anymore.

Think about the little things going on around us every day that show proof of how bad lying and deceitfulness have gotten. Video cameras are showing up everywhere these days because no one can be trusted. Even cops have to wear cameras so that the people they encounter can't lie about dealings with them, and even worse, the cops can't lie about their part in confrontations. Our politicians are constantly being recorded saying one thing and then doing the opposite later. We have been seeing a growing trend in large corporation leaders getting busted for doing dishonest business deals or stealing from their company or from their customers. We are also seeing church leaders preaching and teaching Christian principles in front of the church and then having marital affairs or drug problems when they are not in front of the church. It's everywhere, and it has gotten so bad that it now covers the people that you would never expect it to affect.

I do a lot of interviewing at my job, and it amazes me to see people come in and have an awesome resume filled with what seems to be all kinds of great experience, yet they can't answer simple questions regarding what they say they know. I can usually tell within a few minutes of talking to them if they know what they say they do or if they just lied on their resume to get an interview. Sometimes, if they are really good liars, they will actually get hired, and then you will find out they don't really know what they say they do. It's so bad, though, that you just have to hire the best choice of the liars that you can. Half the time I set up interviews, the people don't even actually show up or even call to tell you they aren't coming. This isn't just a problem in my business; it's everywhere. People just don't have the integrity to do the right thing.

Studies show that 60 percent of adults can't have a ten-minute conversation without lying at least once. When adults have an honesty and integrity problem, you can bet that our children pick up on it, and it teaches them that it's okay. Studies also show that 90 percent of children these days have learned the concept of lying by age four. The bigger problem with this is that when young kids are brought up to think lying is okay, then they start to lie about any and everything. They become compulsive or pathological liars. Normal lying in children is typically done to avoid getting in trouble for something they did or in an attempt to impress other kids, but pathological lying is done for no personal gain. When someone gets so used to lying and becomes pathological with it, they sometimes can't even tell what the truth is and what a lie is anymore. They will get the truth and their lies mixed up and have trouble remembering what they said and who they said it to, and no one will ever trust them. This is what we continue to do to our kids and young people because we have let this struggle become such a big problem.

The scary part about this struggle is that we all know better than to lie and do the wrong things, yet we keep on doing it. I really don't think it was such a big problem in our world even fifteen to twenty years ago. It has just gotten worse and worse. It's no different in that aspect than any of the other struggles we have already talked about, really. It's all because of this Hellven mindset we all have. We feel like we can get away with the little white lies and other things because everyone else is doing them, and there are less and less consequences for things these days.

So what can we do to help stop this trending pattern of deceitfulness? I think we each have to first look at ourselves. We have to make a choice and take a stand to be honest with ourselves first. Ask yourself if you are completely honest in all things with your life. I think we could all be honest and say that we don't put God first. Saying you do but acting like we all act is a complete lie and only adds to the problem. If we all did put God first in our lives, there would be absolutely no reason to write this book because there would be nothing to talk about. It's no coincidence that non-believers say that Christians are the biggest hypocrites. They think that because of our dishonesty to God with how we act like Christians when it's convenient, but act just like non-believers the rest of the time. It is a huge lie and so disrespectful to God. We have to at least stop lying about our relationship with God to ourselves so that we can realize it needs work. Just admitting it to ourselves and asking God for forgiveness will go a long way in helping to eliminate some of the hypocrisy we Christians have created.

We have to then work on our own relationship with

God and get our own families in church and work on it as a family. We have to instill honesty and integrity into our children and make it known that these qualities have to become important again. That may mean some tough love for a while if you have let deceitfulness live in your home for too long, but God will help you and your family overcome it if you are truly taking that stand against it. God will honor you and your family and bless your actions. If every Christian household would just take these steps, even if they are baby steps, we could really turn things around.

After you have worked on yourself and your own honesty and integrity and then gotten your family on board with it, then you can begin to spread these values to other people in your life. Take a stand with it at your job and let your co-workers know that it is important to you. If you are like me and have a leadership role in your company, then you can let all of your employees or potential employees know that honesty and integrity are a must for working there. Make them a core value to your company. People will either tend to take pride in the values, or they will flee from your company because they are not comfortable with the truth. Either way, your company will become better and stronger. If you have friends that don't seem to always be honest, pray about them and then talk to them about it in a loving way and let them know that you would appreciate honesty. Some of these things will be hard if you haven't been honest in the past with the people around you, but again, if you are truly taking the right steps and seeking God in it, He will get you past the obstacles that come up.

I will leave this topic with something we should all remember to use when we struggle with speaking the truth to others. This is an acronym that I came up with to help gain trust from the people in our lives because, without honesty and integrity, we have no trust from others.

Think about what you are going to say before you say it.

Respect others with your words.

Understand how your words can affect others.

Seek God first.

Then speak.

The LORD detests lying lips, but he delights in people who are trustworthy.

Proverbs 12:22

Then you will know the truth, and the truth will set you free.

John 8:32

Finally, brothers and sisters, whatever is true, whatever is noble, whatever is right, whatever is pure, whatever is lovely, whatever is admirable—if anything is excellent or praiseworthy—think about such things.

Whatever you have learned or received or heard from me, or seen in me—put it into practice. And the God of peace will be with you.

Philippians 4:8–9

Whoever walks in integrity walks securely, but whoever takes crooked paths will be found out.

Proverbs 10:9

Therefore each of you must put off falsehood and speak truthfully to your neighbor, for we are all members of one body.

Ephesians 4:25

You, then, who teach others, do you not teach yourself? You who preach against stealing, do you steal? You who say that people should not commit adultery, do you commit adultery? You who abhor idols, do you rob temples? You who boast in the law, do you dishonor God by breaking the law? As it is written: 'God's name is blasphemed among the Gentiles because of you.'

Romans 2:21–24

To do what is right and just is more acceptable to the LORD than sacrifice.

Proverbs 21:3

I know, my God, that you test the heart and are pleased with integrity. All these things I have given willingly and with honest intent. And now I have seen with joy how willingly your people who are here have given to you.

1 Chronicles 29:17

Dear children, let us not love with words or speech but with action and in truth. This is how we know that we belong to the truth and how we set our hearts at rest in his presence.

1 John 3:18–19

For we are taking pains to do what is right, not only in the eyes of the Lord but also in the eyes of man.

2 Corinthians 8:21

WITNESSING

I want to use these last few chapters to talk about some of the struggles we have that are directly related to being a Christian. These will be things we struggle to do because we let the world affect us and sway us from our beliefs. The first one I want to talk about is witnessing.

The very last thing Jesus told the disciples before He ascended to heaven was to go out into the world and witness and proclaim the Gospel. That had to be important if it was going to be the last words He spoke here on earth. It is the number one task we as Christians are supposed to have with our time here, yet not very many of us do it. For the most part, it's because we are Hellven citizens or hypocritical Christians. Like we talked about before, we only act like Christians when we are at church or when it is convenient for us. I'm guilty of it, and I'm sure most of you reading this book are too. It's just what we have become accustomed to and comfortable with.

I think it's sad that the one religion that actually takes witnessing seriously these days, the Jehovah's Witnesses, just gets made fun of for the most part or has door after door slammed in their face. You may not have the same belief system that they have, but I have to commend them for actually doing what they were called to do, unlike most of us Christians. I believe, though, that most of us fear having the same outcome, which would be doors slammed in our faces or being made fun of for trying to witness these days. If not that outcome, then you will be labeled as a "holy roller" by your peers or coworkers at a minimum. Witnessing is also not politically correct these days, and people are cracking down on the separation of church and state and don't want church talk going on outside the church. If you aren't talking "church talk" outside of the church, then what's the point? The people that need to hear it are not in the church.

Think about all of the things in our world that have changed just over the last ten years or so. The world is trying to take God out of everything. The government has tried to take prayer out of our schools and governmental institutions. There is a movement going on to remove all statues and things that are not politically correct from public view, which includes biblical monuments such as the Ten Commandments. This country was founded on biblical and Christian beliefs, yet we continue to try to remove those beliefs from everything we can. We are slowly removing anything and everything that could bear witness. We will soon be to a point where there will be absolutely no witnessing going on unless it comes directly from our mouths, and we will continue to have more regulations on us for that as well. Once God is removed from everything but the church, and we are all taught or forced to leave our "church talk" inside the church, then we are in real trouble.

Let me tell you just how much trouble we are about to be in as things continue to head in the direction we are headed. These are some statistics from Bible.org that should alarm you. Did you know that 95 percent of all Christians have never won a single soul to Christ? Eighty-five percent of all Christians do not consistently witness for Christ. In a survey performed on one particular denomination, 63 percent of church leadership has not one stranger to Jesus in the last two years outside of the church. Eighty-nine percent of the leadership have spent zero time on their list of weekly priorities for going out to evangelize outside the church. All of this is shocking, but especially since 99 percent of the leadership fully believes that every Christian, especially leadership, has been commanded to preach and spread the Gospel to a lost world. We simply have become dependent on the actual church building to be our one and only source of witnessing, which is 100 percent wrong.

Yes, the church is a place that we should be bringing the lost to so that they can be saved, but it should not be what we depend on for our witnessing. For one, if you can't witness outside the church walls, how are you going to get the lost to the church? You have to witness and invite people to the church that you know are lost. They have to see something in you that they want. They have to see that something in you is different than others in the world. That in itself is a challenge as we have already talked about us being hypocrites to the world.

All of these things going on in the world around us are what makes witnessing so hard and uncomfortable. We fear that we will be rejected, made fun of, or condemned for "pushing" our beliefs on others. The easy choice is to just stay quiet and leave the witnessing to the staff at our local churches. Well, I think we all do that, but I think we are all smart enough to know that it's not right or what God has commanded us to do.

So, because I am in this boat, I don't even begin to act like I have the answers to this struggle, but I do know where to look for help, and that is God and His Word. Just like most of the other struggles we have talked about, seeking God should always be the first step. If you really want to make a difference in your own witnessing, or start it for the first time, start praying about it. In your daily prayers, begin to ask God for peace and comfort in your mind and ask Him to take your anxiety about witnessing away. Ask Him to give you opportunities and the words to say when those opportunities arise. Be intentional and direct with what you ask in your prayers and conversations with the Lord, and He will open the doors and reveal the perfect opportunities to you. It will seem like He is bringing the lost to you, and all you have to do is open your mouth and let the Lord speak through you. I fully believe God will give you easy and comfortable situations for your first few times if you are truly seeking Him in prayer about wanting to get on track with your witnessing, so seek Him first.

Next, once you have prayed for courage and opportunities, get out there and keep an eye out for situations or people that are obviously needing help or hurting. God will put you in front of the lost on a daily basis when you are seeking Him, but you have to be ready at all times. You can start with simple things like asking someone if you can pray for them. Most people, even lost, will almost always have something going on in their lives that they won't turn down prayers for. My dad did this thing when he and my mom went out to eat at restaurants. Right after he would order his food, he always asked the waiter or waitress if he could pray for them. If they said yes, he would ask them if they had anything specific going on that he could pray for, and then he prayed for them. I witnessed it several times, and you can just see the people light up. I have seen some of them cry and have even seen some of them tell my dad how much they needed that. Just something small like that is easy to do, but it takes being bold and just taking that first step and opening your mouth. You can also be on the lookout for opportunities to invite people to your church, which is another simple but more comfortable way to witness. You can simply ask someone if they go to church. If they say no, then tell them about your church and let them know that you would be glad to take them. You don't have to be pushy; just let them know that you would love to bring them and let them know how much the church helps you with things going on in your life. Even if you aren't comfortable enough yet to fully witness, just getting the lost to the church is a good step, and by inviting them, you play a part in leading them to the Lord.

I will tell you that I am in my mid-forties, and I was saved at the age of eight, and I can only count a few times in my life where I sat someone down and fell like I personally led them to the Lord. I have always tried to invite people to church or done some indirect witnessing, but I have never been bold enough or comfortable enough to just openly witness fully to strangers or even friends, for that matter. The one thing I can tell you, though, is that those few times where I did made me feel so good and so fulfilled. I think every soul you can win for the Lord is the greatest accomplishment you can have here on earth, more than any worldly thing you could ever do. It feels so great, has the greatest reward, and is really the easiest thing you can do, so we should surely do it more often.

There are roughly 7.4 billion people in the world. Christianity is by far the largest religion in the world, with just over 2.2 billion followers. Look at those figures and just think about what we as Christians could do if we each just lead a single soul each year to Christ. Some of us go a lifetime of being a Christian and not winning one soul, so I challenge you to set a goal to win at least one per year for your remaining life. That is obviously not a goal that God would set for us, but I just want you to think about all of these things and make an effort, which is more than most of us are doing. If we all started taking small steps like these, then we could see a real turnaround in our world. The fact is that unless we quit taking God out of our world, and allow Him back in it, then we are facing even harder times, and we should all be doing everything in our power to keep others from suffering the wrath that is coming one day.

Life is just a blink in the eyes of eternity. Once our time here is up, there are only two options for every soul: heaven or hell. There is no Hellven. The things we can accomplish here or the riches we can gather can't be taken with us when we die, but the souls we win in our time here will be rewarded for eternity. Let's all care a little less about what is cool or what is politically correct and care more about what truly counts in this world and win souls for Christ with every chance we are given.

> *Then Jesus came to them and said, 'All authority in heaven and on earth has been given to me. Therefore go and make disciples of all nations, baptizing them in the name of the Father and of the Son and of the Holy Spirit, and teaching them to obey everything I have commanded you. And surely I am with you always, to the very end of the age.'*
>
> **Matthew 28:18–20**

In the same way, let your light shine before others, that they may see your good deeds and glorify your Father in heaven.

Matthew 5:16

But you will receive power when the Holy Spirit comes on you; and you will be my witnesses in Jerusalem, and in all Judea and Samaria, and to the ends of the earth.

Acts 1:8

He said to them, 'Go into all the world and preach the gospel to all creation.'

Mark 16:15

'You are my witnesses,' declares the LORD, 'and my servant whom I have chosen, so that you may know and believe me and understand that I am he. Before me no god was formed, nor will there be one after me.'

Isaiah 43:10

How, then, can they call on the one they have not believed in? And how can they believe in the one of whom they have not heard? And how can they hear without someone preaching to them? And how can anyone preach unless they are sent? As it is written: 'How beautiful are the feet of those who bring good news!'

Romans 10:14–15

Let us not become weary of doing good, for at the proper time we will reap a harvest if we do not give up. Therefore, as we have opportunity, let us do good to all people, especially to those who belong to the family of believers.

Galatians 6:9–10

So do not be ashamed of the testimony about our Lord or of me his prisoner. Rather, join with me in suffering for the gospel, by the power of God. He has saved us and called us to a holy life—not because of anything we have done but because of his own purpose and grace. This grace was given us in Christ Jesus before the beginning of time.

2 Timothy 1:8–9

Because we have heard of your faith in Christ Jesus and of the love you have for all God's people—the faith and love that spring from the hope stored up for you in heaven and about which you have already heard in the true message of the gospel that has come to you. In the same way, the gospel is bearing fruit and growing throughout the whole world—just as it has been doing among you since the day you heard it and truly understood God's grace.

Colossians 1:4–6

But you are a chosen people, a royal priesthood, a holy nation, God's special possession, that you may declare the praises of him who called you out of darkness into his wonderful light.

1 Peter 2:9

OBEDIENCE TO GOD

If you are like me and living as a citizen of Hellven and not living your life fully for God, then being obedient to Him can be extra hard. The problem with obedience when you are not living fully for God is that you tend to tune God out and not listen to Him. You will find yourself listening to the world and to the people around you. Satan will use whatever and whoever he can to distract you from a calling or instructions from God.

Look back at my introduction to this book and remember where I talk about how long it took me to be obedient to God in writing this book. I struggled with it for several years before I took it seriously and got this book going, and was consistently working on it. When you start being obedient, the next thing you have to watch for is Satan and the world turning their efforts from distraction to doubt. You will find yourself fighting your own doubts, and you just have to push through them. Even as I started truly working on the book, I would find times where I would be looking for things to write, and I would tell myself, *What are you even doing? You aren't qualified to be writing a book*, but I kept on pushing. One week I had even taken a couple of days off from my writing out of my own discouragement and doubt, and I got a word from God in church that very next Sunday. We had a guest speaker, which was good, but I am partial to my own church pastor, so I found myself drifting in thought and not fully paying attention. All of a sudden, it's like I heard a loud snap, and the next words I heard was the speaker saying, "Sometimes simply being willing to be obedient for something that you don't feel you are qualified for automatically qualifies you." I thought, *Wow*, what an amazing way to look at things, especially as I struggled with my qualifications for writing a book. There were just too many things that God put out there for me, resources He gave me, chances He gave me, and subtle things He would speak to me about to continue doubting that He called me to write this book.

We have to listen to hear God, though. We have to truly be open to what He wants to tell us, and we have to open our hearts to Him. His instructions or words can be something very simple that He wants you to know or do, or they can be huge, life-changing things for you. The big things are not easy, as they can bring on all kinds of obstacles and issues, but the little things can also be just as hard to be obedient in when you are not living right with God.

I want to share another very personal experience I had in being obedient to God in a small thing. I say small because it was simply just telling someone something, but it would turn out to be a huge blessing. This happened a few years ago. I have two older sisters and one younger brother, and at that point in our lives, we all had multiple kids except my older sister, who was on the verge of turning forty and has still not been able to have a child. She had been to several doctors and tried many things over the years. She had even gotten pregnant and had miscarriages. Well, on Mother's Day in 2013, I found myself sitting beside her in church. The preacher was doing his typical Mother's Day spill and recognizing all of the mothers there that day. I remember looking over at her and seeing tears roll down her cheeks as that particular day was hard for her as she wanted to be a mother herself so badly. Right then and there, I just asked God, "Why can't she be blessed with a child, Lord?" Suddenly, everything and every noise in the room stopped as if it all froze and plain as day I heard the voice of God as if He was standing right in front of me say, "Tell her that she will have a child before the next Mother's Day." It still gives me chills as I am typing it right now because it was so real and awesome. Honestly, it freaked me out because, at that point, I had never really heard God speak so directly to me in my life. I left church that day without saying a word to her. I thought that if I told her something as bold as that and it did not come true that it would just crush her even worse. I struggled with it all day long until I finally had to tell someone, so I told my wife. She began to cry herself and demanded that I call my sister immediately. Sometimes, being obedient helps when you have a threatening wife, LOL, but I still had to decide to do it on my own. It was just telling her something, but it was still very hard because of the doubt I let creep in. Finally, late that evening, I called my sister. I told her exactly what happened and what I heard. I told her that I did not want to upset her but that I just felt like I needed to be obedient in what I was told to tell her. She took it fine and thanked me for telling her, but as we hung up, I got a sense that she doubted it herself. A couple of months passed, and I got a phone call from my sister one day. I answered, and she sounded all excited. She told me that she had gone to the doctor that day and they were about to start her on some new fertilization medicine and that as part of getting on it, she had to take a pregnancy test, which she did, and she was pregnant! It was completely awesome. She even told me I was her first phone call because of what I had told her. The next few months were a little nerve-racking, but God's words were true, and on the next April 28, my sister gave birth to a healthy baby boy. That was two weeks before Mother's Day! Praise God!

I will tell you; I am no saint and nothing special. I don't do a good job of living each day for the Lord. I fail at it all the time. I am a hypocrite and a sinner. There is no special reason that God told me to share that news with my sister, other than He wanted me to be obedient. The great news for you and me, though, is that if you find yourself not living for God but rather for this world, our God is gracious. He is forgiving and loving. All you have to do is ask for forgiveness and let God transform you, and you will be able to get back on an obedient path. God will forget your disobedience and give you an obedient heart. He promises this is His word. He will give you more and more opportunities to be obedient, and it will bless your life as well as those around you.

There is no better feeling than to know you were obedient and pleased the Lord. As I am getting close to finishing this book, I just printed everything I had done so that my wife could start reading it and letting me know what she thinks about it. As I pulled the first group of sheets out of my printer and I saw the cover page on paper, I just about lost it. I was overcome with emotion and joy and could sense God telling me He was proud of me for being obedient. I have an awesome sense of accomplishment, unlike anything I could do on a worldly level. I feel like I have made my heavenly Father proud, and there is nothing that compares to that feeling. Remembering that feeling makes the next time He asks you to do something a lot easier. Again, whatever He chooses to do with this book is completely up to Him, and I have at least done my part.

> *Why do you call me, 'Lord, Lord,' and do not do what I say? As for everyone who comes to me and hears my words and puts them into practice, I will show you what they are like. They are like a man building a house, who dug down deep and laid the foundation on rock. When a flood came, the torrent struck that house but could not shake it, because it was*

well built. But the one who hears my words and does not put them into practice is like a man who built a house on the ground without a foundation. The moment the torrent struck that house, it collapsed and its destruction was complete.

Luke 6:46–49

Another reason I wrote you was to see if you would stand the test and be obedient in everything.

2 Corinthians 2:9

And we know that in all things God works for the good of those who love him, who have been called according to his purpose.

Romans 8:28

Son though he was, he learned obedience from what he suffered and, once made perfect, he became the source of eternal salvation for all who obey him.

Hebrews 5:8–9

Trust in the LORD with all your heart and lean not on your own understanding; in all your ways submit to him, and he will make your paths straight.

Proverbs 3:5–6

If you fully obey the LORD your God and carefully follow all his commands I give you today, the LORD your God will set you high above all the nations on earth. All these blessings will come on you and accompany you if you obey the LORD your God.

Deuteronomy 28:1–2

Whatever you do, work at it with all your heart, as working for the Lord, not for human masters, since you know that you will receive an inheritance from the Lord as a reward. It is the Lord Christ you are serving.

Colossians 3:23–24

No, the word is very near you; it is in your mouth and in your heart so you may obey it.

Deuteronomy 30:14

Now if you obey me fully and keep my covenant, then out of all nations you will be my treasured possession. Although the whole earth is mine.

Exodus 19:5

Jesus replied, 'Anyone who loves me will obey my teaching. My Father will love them, and we will come to them and make our home with them.'

John 14:23

CONVICTION AND REPENTANCE

When we are truly saved, we are filled with the Holy Spirit, which is part of the Trinity; the Father, the Son, and the Spirit. God sent the Holy Spirit to convict the world of our sins. The Bible talks about this in John, chapter 16. The Holy Spirit is what guides you through things in your life and who helps you do the things we are supposed to do as Christians. We still have to make the choice to allow the Spirit to move in us and control our paths, though. When we are walking closely along the path that the Spirit sets out for us, conviction comes to us naturally, but when we stray from that path, we lose our sense of conviction, and that is, unfortunately, where most of us are these days. We are off of our path, being led blindly by the world and without conviction.

Conviction is actually one of the main ways you can know that you are truly saved as a Christian. Romans 3:23 says, "For all have sinned," and we all have,

Christian or not. We also all know right from wrong, Christian or not. Once you become a Christian, though, there is a difference in you when you sin. You don't just have the normal guilty feeling in your gut and mind like a normal person with decent standards; there is something different about that feeling. It's deeper than your conscience. When you sin as a Christian, you feel it in your soul, and it weighs on you unlike anything else. Conviction is an overwhelming sense of wrong in your heart. If you feel these things when you know you have sinned, then you can know that it is the Holy Spirit moving in your heart and soul. He is making sure you are aware of the wrong you have done so that you can seek repentance and forgiveness of your sins. If you do not feel conviction when you sin, then you need to decide if you truly surrendered your heart to the Lord and are saved, or you have let so much sin creep into your life that you have allowed your heart to harden and build up a barrier from the Holy Spirit that you need to remove.

Most of us Christians are here in Hellven with hardened hearts, and we just can't feel or hear the Holy Spirit anymore. That is one of the biggest problems with Christianity these days. We don't have conviction, which leads to a bigger sin problem, which is only adding fuel to the wildfire that is spreading across the world. Without conviction, there is no one asking for repentance either, which means that the hardening of our hearts just grows stronger. Can you see Satan fanning the flames?

We as Christians need to snap out of it and get back

to a point where we can allow the Holy Spirit to move in us again. We first have to allow ourselves to remember what it feels like to be convicted. We have to get back to a point where we remember how much our sins dishonor God. We have to remember that Jesus was convicted of all the sins of the world and took our punishment, and died for our sins. Remember Him on the cross and how much He suffered for us. Go watch *Passion of the Christ* or anything you can do to refresh your memory about the ultimate conviction of sin, and then see if your heart begins to soften. Sometimes we need a good reminder because we have let ourselves slip so far away from the truth. Do whatever you can to open your heart back up to the Holy Spirit so you can begin to feel that conviction again. We all have to realize that we are the ones who moved, not Jesus, and not the Holy Spirit. They are constantly there where we left them and built up soundproof walls around them. Begin to break down those walls piece by piece.

Once you can begin to feel and hear the Holy Spirit again, you will again be able to have conviction in your heart and soul. When you get to that point, you next need to seek repentance, not only for the sins you are being convicted of but repentance for slipping so far out of tune with the Lord. True repentance is recognizing our sins based on our convictions, deciding to turn away from those sins, and avoiding the same sins again. Repentance is also regretting that you ever did the sinful things and regretting that you have hurt or shamed God.

The awesome thing about repentance, though, is that you only have to open your mouth and heart and simply ask God to forgive you for your sins. There are no other special tasks you have to perform or no works that you have to do. It's simply asking and then receiving His forgiveness. The Bible teaches us that God instantly forgives and then forgets our sins when we repent.

Conviction and repentance must be a part of our daily lives as Christians, period. Even in the craziness of this world that we live in every day, we have to remember these two very important things and apply them. Just keep in mind that we serve an awesome God, and no matter what we do or how many times we do it, He is willing and ready to forgive us every single time. Sin is in our nature, and we will spend our entire lives struggling with it, but as long as we are seeking God, the Holy Spirit will be there to guide us, and God will be with us each step of the way to forgive us.

> *When he comes, he will prove the world to be in the wrong about sin and righteousness and judgment.*
>
> **John 16:8**
>
> *When the people heard this, they were cut to the heart and said to Peter and the other apostles, 'Brothers, what shall we do?' Peter replied, 'Repent and be baptized, every one of you, in the name of Jesus Christ for the*

forgiveness of your sins. And you will receive the gift of the Holy Spirit.'

Acts 2:37–38

But because of your stubbornness and your unrepentant heart, you are storing up wrath against yourself for the day of God's wrath, when his righteous judgment will be revealed. God 'will repay each person according to what they have done.'

Romans 2:5–6

Jesus answered them, 'It is not the healthy who need a doctor, but the sick. I have not come to call the righteous, but sinners to repentance.'

Luke 5:31–32

Repent, then, and turn to God, so that your sins may be wiped out, that times of refreshing may come from the Lord.

Acts 3:19

If my people, who are called by my name, will humble themselves and pray and seek my face and turn from their wicked ways, then I will hear from heaven, and I will forgive their sin and will heal their land.

2 Chronicles 7:14

I tell you that in the same way there will be more rejoicing in heaven over one sinner who repents than over ninety-nine righteous persons who do not need to repent.

Luke 15:7

The Lord is not slow in keeping his promise, as some understand slowness. Instead he is patient with you, not wanting anyone to perish, but everyone to come to repentance.

2 Peter 3:9

You have no part or share in this ministry, because your heart is not right before God. Repent of this wickedness and pray to the Lord in the hope that he may forgive you for having such a thought in your heart. For I see that you are full of bitterness and captive to sin.

Acts 8:21–23

DENOUNCING YOUR "HELLVEN" CITIZENSHIP

There is only one way we as Christians can turn things around in this world we live in, and that is for us all to begin to denounce our citizenship to Hellven. In other words, we all need to work on not being lukewarm Christians or only being Christians when it is convenient to us. We need to quit being hypocrites all the time. We need to take a stand and put God first in our own lives and then begin to put God back in control of the things of this world. Otherwise, this world is headed for doom and destruction, and we have only scratched the surface of how bad it will get.

When someone has an addiction, they truly never get freed from that addiction until they fully commit to changing and turn completely away from their addiction. They chose to no longer live as a slave to that addiction and have a life change that can easily be seen by everyone around them. In the same exact manner, we have to fully commit to a true life change in our Christian walks. We have to decide that the things of this world are no longer going to hold us captive and control us. We have to choose that we are no longer going to let others influence us or be embarrassed to be Christians around our peers. That true change has to begin with you and me.

We are always going to have these struggles we have talked about in our lives. That is not going to change, but we have to change the way we think and react to the struggles. We have to get our minds right to begin to see any changes in our hearts and actions. We have to try to block out all of the negative and sinful thoughts and replace those with positive things. Philippians 4:8 tells us this, "Finally, brothers and sisters, whatever is true, whatever is noble, whatever is right, whatever is pure, whatever is lovely, whatever is admirable—if anything is excellent or praiseworthy—think about such things." The Bible is full of verses that teach us to put our thoughts and minds on the right things instead of the things of this world. Once we can begin to do so, then we can get focused on making bigger changes in our lives to help us with our struggles and strengthen our relationship again with God, which will help get us back on track.

It's real easy to hit our "Christian" power button and talk about all of these practices to overcome these worldly struggles, but it's even harder to actually put them into action in our daily lives. Once you have lived in the world for so long, acting like someone you are not, it will take just as long, if not longer, to overcome the reputation you have made for yourself. People will accuse you of being fake. They will make fun of you and call you a "holy roller." They will think you have lost your mind. Just remember that those people still have their blinders on and do not see how you see and that it is your job to be the light for them.

Make a commitment with me to work on how we as Christians deal with all of the struggles we have talked about in this book and the many others we face daily. Let's make a commitment to help stop the hypocritical stigma that has been placed on Christians today by acting like we have been changed and doing what we have been called to do, even when it is not to our benefit here in the world. Let's work on these small things and see if we can start to make big changes in this world.

> *But our citizenship is in heaven. And we eagerly await a Savior from there, the Lord Jesus Christ, who, by the power that enables him to bring everything under his control, will transform our lowly bodies so that they will be like his glorious body.*
>
> **Philippians 3:20–21**

> *Do not conform to the pattern of this world, but be transformed by the renewing of your mind. Then you will be able to test and approve what God's will is—his good, pleasing and perfect will.*
>
> **Romans 12:2**

If the world hates you, keep in mind that it hated me first. If you belonged to the world, it would love you as its own. As it is, you do not belong to the world, but I have chosen you out of the world. That is why the world hates you.

John 15:18–19

Set your minds on things above, not on earthly things.

Colossians 3:2

My prayer is not that you take them out of the world but that you protect them from the evil one. They are not of the world, even as I am not of it.

John 17:15–16

Dear friends, I urge you, as foreigners and exiles, to abstain from sinful desires, which wage war against your soul. Live such good lives among the pagans that, though they accuse you of doing wrong, they may see your good deeds and glorify God on the day he visits us.

1 Peter 2:11–12

Do not love the world or anything in the world. If anyone loves the world, love for the Father is not in them. For everything in the world—the lust of the flesh, the lust of the eyes, and the pride of life—comes not from the Father but from the world. The world and its desires pass away, but whoever does the will of God lives forever.

1 John 2:15–17

I have come into the world as a light, so that no one who believes in me should stay in darkness.

John 12:46

But if we walk in the light, as he is in the light, we have fellowship with one another, and the blood of Jesus, his Son, purifies us from all sin.

1 John 1:7

For the grace of God has appeared that offers salvation to all people. It teaches us to say 'No' to ungodliness and worldly passions, and to live self-controlled, upright and godly lives in this present age, while we wait for the blessed hope—the appearing of the glory of our great God and Savior, Jesus Christ, who gave himself for us to redeem us from all wickedness and to purify for himself a people that are his very own, eager to do what is good.

Titus 2:11–14

CPSIA information can be obtained
at www.ICGtesting.com
Printed in the USA
BVHW090024110522
636630BV00010B/1028